D0876384

Mahatma Gandhi

The Great Soul

IMMORTALS OF HISTORY

Mahatma Gandhi

The Great Soul

by Emil Lengyel

Franklin Watts, Inc.
575 Lexington Avenue
New York, N.Y. 10022

To Ana Celia and Hilli
with fraternal affection

SECOND PRINTING

Copyright © 1966 by Franklin Watts, Inc.
Library of Congress Catalog Card Number: 67–10167
Printed in the United States of America

Contents

Contents

Mahatma Gandhi

The Great Soul

Prologue

Jawaharlal Nehru, the first prime minister of India, died in 1964, leaving behind a country founded upon the principles of *ahimsa* (uh-*him*-suh), no violence. That same year, Martin Luther King, Jr., an American Negro, received the Nobel Peace Prize for his work against racial discrimination in the United States by nonviolent means. In 1961, Albert John Luthuli was awarded the Nobel Peace Prize for his nonviolent crusades against South African policies of discrimination.

In a true sense, these leaders, and others, were and are disciples of one man, Mohandas Karamchand Gandhi, an Indian Hindu. Throughout a long and dedicated life, until his death in 1948, Gandhi preached his belief in *satyagraha* (sut-yuh-*gruh*-huh), truth force. He proclaimed that truth was the only effective force to combat evil, and that violence could never bring justice. His name became synonymous with nonviolent methods of fighting injustice throughout the world.

1

Mahatma Gandhi: The Great Soul

Mohandas Gandhi, called the *Mahatma* (Great Soul),
had no official government position in his country. He
did not found a religion, nor did he claim to be a religious
leader. His physical appearance was unimpressive, and he
was a poor public speaker. Yet the voice of no other twentieth-century man has been heard by so many millions of
people. Great leaders and starved peasants alike listened
to his words. He left behind him a goal which the world
is still trying to achieve.

1

About a Shy Boy

The voice of the child sounded shrilly.

"*Ba, ba* (mother, mother), hurry, please do. The sun is out; it really is. Now you can have your meal."

As fast as a gazelle of the Himalaya Mountains, Putlibai Gandhi rushed out of the house into the courtyard, her brown sari billowing as a sudden gust of wind tugged at the folds of the loosely draped garment. She had unusually large dark eyes, a finely chiseled nose, and a firm chin. Her pinched lips indicated a woman of strong character. She was in her early thirties, but showed no signs of age. Although Indian women aged quickly, Putlibai had still retained her youthful freshness.

As she ran into the open, she panted, "The sun? Let me see!"

But the sun was no longer visible. It was hidden behind

3

a black cloud that covered the patch of blue out of which it had blazed a minute before.

The child was crestfallen.

"It was out; I'm telling you it was. But now it is gone."

As suddenly as the sun had vanished, a solid sheet of mist now darkened the yard. Heavy raindrops began a continuous barrage on the tin-foiled eaves. This was an outburst of the monsoon, the seasonal rain of India, which gusted inland from the nearby seashore. The pounding waves of the sea outthundered the drumming rain on the eaves.

Even though the child was disappointed, his mother looked cheerful.

"Never mind, child, this rain was needed, and it is a blessing. It will help our people to have food. What matter if I do not eat today."

The child who had urged his mother to eat was Mohandas Karamchand Gandhi, a small, six-year-old boy with big dark eyes—"the eyes of a doe," his mother would say affectionately. He had a drooping nose and large ears tilting away from his head.

The Gandhis lived in the town of Porbandar, way up the western coast of India, on the Kathiawar peninsula jutting into the Arabian Sea. The year was 1875.

Putlibai Gandhi had made a vow never to eat when the face of the sun was hidden. This was her sacrifice to the gods—the Hindu gods of India. It was an appeal that asked the gods to be kind to her family, and to her neighbors less fortunate than she, whose larders were empty when the monsoon rains failed.

Hinduism, the religion of the Gandhis and of most of their neighbors, had many practices which seemed strange to Western man. It was difficult to know what sacrifice the Hindu gods expected—there were so many of them. Some learned men said that there were forty *crores* of gods. Since one crore alone is ten million, that added up to four hundred million dwellers of the Hindu heaven. But Putlibai thought that Vishnu the preserver was a particularly mighty god, and she hoped that he would preserve her family in good health. She made her vows to him.

Porbandar, where Mohandas was born, is a lovely town when seen from a distance. It is built on a sloping shore, pounded by the Arabian Sea. The house of the Gandhi family was near the water, and, as a child, Mohandas was fascinated by the deep growling sound of the amethyst-colored sea. Which of the forty crores of gods moved the sea? he wondered. And what was beyond the great expanse of water? Was it another land, and if so, who lived there? Was it inhabited by terrible monsters who devoured people, as a friend had said? Or was it another India, with more food for the poor people? And how far away was the land from which the Britishers had come—those people with pink cheeks who were the masters of India. Some people said that Britain was always wrapped in gloom; that there the sun never shone; that it was always cold; and that its people would have died if they had not maintained their strength by eating beef. That thought made the child shiver because he—like other Hindus—never ate meat. Mohandas often thought about these lands beyond the sea. Would he ever see them?

The young boy liked to stand on the shore. It was lined with lovely palms planted by a long-ago prince. The trees had gnarled trunks, and fastened to them were the sturdy boats of the local fishermen who sometimes returned to Porbandar with bucketfuls of fish. But sometimes they did not return, and then there was sadness in the town for the lost breadwinners. And sometimes the fish did not fill the waters and then, too, there was moaning in the alleys, the moaning of people who had no food.

Mohandas liked to roam in the maze of Porbandar's alleys. He was well known to the townspeople, and his family was respected. His favorite place was the busy bazaar, the marketplace bustling with life. He liked to watch the artisans sitting cross-legged in their cubbyholes which were scooped out of the porous soil, chattering away as they used their small hammers on silver and tinware.

Mohandas was particularly entranced by the haggling in the artisans' lanes. A potential buyer might ask the price of a pewter drinking cup. The artisan would quote the price, to which the buyer would react with scornful laughter.

6

"I did not ask for the price of the crown jewels of the maharaja of Kathiawar," he would roar. "I asked merely about the price of this mean little cup."

Then the haggling would begin in earnest. After some time an agreement would be reached, far below the artisan's beginning price. Mohandas soon learned that such verbal clashes were considered important parts of bazaar life, appreciated by buyer and seller alike.

In the bazaar and away from it, Porbandar looked little different from India's 600,000 other villages and towns. People lived in huts made of mud bricks or wattle—a material of branches and reeds—topped off with straw roofs to protect the dwellers from the weather. The thatched roofs gave off a sweetish odor of decomposition, caused by the burning sun on the rain-soaked straw.

Mohandas saw little of the insides of these windowless huts. His parents had warned him to keep away from them, for they were the homes of lower-caste people. Contact with the lower caste was considered defiling by members of higher castes. However, since the huts had only doorways, Mohandas sometimes managed to peek into them. They were dark, with walls blackened by smoke. There were hardly any furnishings: a few pots and jugs, but no beds or chairs—people rested on the bare floors. Invariably there were people in the huts, the old and the very young. At the age of thirty, people were old—and most of them died before then. They died of many diseases—particularly malaria and bubonic plague—

which constantly ravaged the Indian countryside. Sometimes people died for lack of food.

Young Mohandas had seen many people die of starvation. It was so common that he considered it a natural cause of death. And he never asked the reason. He assumed that it was the will of one of the forty crores of gods, and besides it was not in the Indian nature to ask such questions.

Starvation came mostly when Porbandar seemed at its best, when Mohandas was not driven inside by the rain that poured endlessly out of the blackened sky—the monsoon. Sometimes the rains were late, and at other times they did not come at all. Then the sky was so blue that young Mohandas thought he could see some of the gods frolicking in the heavens. (He assumed that the gods had a good time in the same way he did—by playing.) However, when the skies remained too beautiful during the monsoon season, Mohandas knew that many people would leave their earthly lives because of the famine resulting from no rain. But he did not worry. He was sure that no living creature ever died. He believed—as did other Hindus—in the *samsara*, the transmigration of the soul. If a person appeared to have died—of starvation, for instance—his death was not real. If he had been good to his family, he would become a mighty prince after this so-called death, with plenty to eat and wearing diamond-studded clothes. But if the person had been bad to his children, then he would become a loathsome creature, perhaps a scorpion or a snake.

About a Shy Boy

Young Mohandas was as certain about other things in his life as he was of the samsara. He knew that he could play with some children, but not with others. He might play with children who belonged to a higher caste than he, if they were willing to play with him. And he could play with children of his own caste. The caste system of India's Hindus had been introduced into the country ages before. Once the caste had served as a mutual-help association against the demands of more powerful groups. In the course of time, however, it became organized discrimination. Only members of the same caste could intermarry, dine with one another—interdine—or have intimate dealings.

There are four main castes in India, and within these, hundreds of subcastes. The highest caste is that of the Brahmans (BRAH-mans), the priestly people "who have knowledge." If they are faithful to their Hindu creed, they must lead an isolated life, communicating only with their own kind. Next are the Kshatriyas (KSHAT-treyas), those who rule. The third caste is the Vaisyas (VISE-yas), or merchants, to which Mohandas belonged. His subcaste was the Bania, or traders. His ancestors had been grocers. The fourth caste is the Sudras (SOO-dras), or servants. They clean houses, tend the fields, and perform other such tasks.

There was no ironbound separation among members of the castes. Mohandas' kinsfolk, for instance, were prime ministers of princely states, even though they belonged to the traders' class. But Mohandas was warned

9

to keep out of the quarters of people who lived in darkness, who did not belong to any caste, and were therefore called outcastes, or untouchables. These people were restricted in their occupations. They could only do work that members of the castes considered defiling, as, for instance, hauling away dead animals or cleaning latrines.

Outcastes were not allowed to enter the temples of the caste Hindus, nor to draw water from the common well. They had separate wells and separate shrines (*haveli*). When walking on the road, they had to give warning to caste Hindus to get out of the way because their very shadows were considered unclean. If an outcaste's shadow fell on a caste Hindu, the latter had to perform an elaborate ritual of purification. If the shadow fell on a caste Hindu's food, the food was thought to be polluted and had to be thrown away.

So widespread was the caste system that there were higher and lower classes even among the outcastes. The lowest were those who washed other outcastes' clothes. In some regions these people were not allowed even to show their faces by day, so that they became nocturnal creatures, stirring only when others were asleep.

The members of the different castes were not distinguished by the colors of their skins or by special clothing. Then how did people know the way to treat their neighbors? Everybody knew everyone else's caste in India's hundreds of thousands of hamlets. Only in bigger cities was it at all possible to escape the heavy hand of custom.

Even in the India of today, where the constitution has outlawed the caste system, it is still much in force. Changes are occurring, however, although it is very difficult to change age-old habits of living.

Young Mohandas Gandhi, of the Vaisya caste, spoke *Gujarati*, the native language throughout a large segment of India, extending from the Arabian Sea for hundreds of miles inland. There are more than seven hundred languages and important dialects on the subcontinent. Gujarati, one of the major languages, is Indo-European, as is English, but it is closer to Sanskrit, the parent of all these tongues, in which the most important Hindu sacred scripts were written. When Mohandas Gandhi grew to manhood, he mixed his Gujarati with other Indian languages, such as Hindi, the most important of them all. But by that time it made no difference what language he spoke or if he was understood. People venerated him whether or not he spoke at all.

Mohandas did not live in the type of house which he saw all around him. His home was made of stone, with two floors for the family, and small chambers under the roof for the servants. This was the house of Mohandas' father, who was a *dewan*, or prime minister.

Today the title of prime minister usually indicates a country's head of government. But Karamchand Gandhi was not the leader of an entire nation. He was head of government of a small Indian state.

There were 562 such states at that time, and they

formed the "India of the Princes." Native princes ruled in these areas, although the real power was in the hands of the British, who ran the vast subcontinent with its hundreds of millions of people. There was also British India, containing the larger portion of the Indian people, which Britain ruled directly.

There was a particularly large number of native princes on the Kathiawar peninsula. The territory had 21,000 square miles, about the size of the state of West Virginia, and contained 193 principalities. Some of them were little more than crossroad villages; for instance, Gandhol was inhabited by only 137 people. The British could have done away with such states, of course, but they did not, because it served their interests to retain the princes. This helped to create the impression that Indians were ruled by fellow Indians. Also, the British could play on the princes' jealousies, and keep the real power in their own hands.

The parents of Karamchand Gandhi—grandparents of Mohandas—had guessed correctly when they named their child Karamchand, which means "man of action." He was precisely that. An impressive-looking person, he was able to get important jobs. However, he was not an educated man. Reading was not his strong point, and writing even less. He did manage to read simple sentences and could write his name. But the prime minister of an Indian state did not need to acquire such skills. He had plenty of scribes who could do the writing for him. The prime minister was expected to have strength and common sense, both of which Karamchand Gandhi possessed.

Father Gandhi considered himself a religious Hindu although he had no religious training. He visited the temples and listened to learned discourses about religion. Later in life, when he learned to read a little, he liked to study one of the holiest Hindu scripts, the *Bhagavad Gita*. It contains what is considered the substance of the creed, the Hindu equivalent of the Christian Sermon on the Mount. It concerns the warrior Arjuna and the divine Krishna, who was serving as a charioteer on the eve of a great battle. Revealing his true nature, Krishna showed to Arjuna that truth was the greatest good and that salvation could be reached by intellectual effort, honest action, and devotion to the gods' laws. Later in his life, Karamchand Gandhi would daily repeat aloud some of the verses of the *Gita*.

The prime minister married four times, having lost three wives through early deaths. He had two daughters from his first and second marriages, none from the third, and a daughter and three sons from the fourth. Mohandas was the youngest. His mother Putlibai was eighteen years younger than his father. She was twenty-eight when Mohandas was born on October 2, 1869, while Karamchand was forty-six, an advanced age in the India of that time.

Mohandas recalled in later years that Karamchand was "truthful, brave, generous, but short-tempered." Being a man of some importance, he seldom smiled. There was a saying in those days: "Don't trust smiling people. They want something from you."

Karamchand Gandhi served several princes in the capacity of minister and prime minister. One of these was Raj Sahib, prince of the Wankaner state, which contained only 415 square miles. Even though the state was tiny, the prince was powerful, having the right of life and death over his subjects. The decline of population in Wankaner within a ten-year period, about the time that Karamchand Gandhi served the prince, indicates the awesome problems which rulers faced in that part of the world. Normally populations will increase due to the excess of births over deaths. But in this state—as in many other Indian states—the population often decreased. In ten years, Wankaner's population fell from 39,300 to 27,300, due to famine. One of these famine years was known as "rat year"; and an appalling year it was.

"The rats appeared suddenly in dense masses past all counting," a British army captain of the Indian forces reported, "as if springing from the earth, about the harvest season. Nothing could stop them—fire ditches had been tried in vain; they moved along, a mighty host, eating up all that came in their way. Then, all at once they vanished, as if by magic, and for years not one was to be seen. They were about double the size of the common rat, and were of reddish sandy color."

Where starvation is common, one would expect a high

rate of crime because people will try to keep alive by stealing. Strangely, this was not the case. Records show that in the entire state there was only one jail "with a daily average of five prisoners." Of course, the explanation may be that there was nothing to steal.

Father Gandhi was dewan of Rajkot, too. It had a smaller territory than Wankaner—282 square miles—but a larger population, perhaps because it suffered less from famine. It is not likely that a minister was well paid, since the average annual revenue of this entire state, for instance, amounted to only seven thousand dollars.

Karamchand Gandhi also aided the ruler of Porbandar, where Mohandas was born. This was the largest of the states that he served. It also had the largest decline in population, from 103,000 inhabitants to 70,000 within a single decade, again because of famine. Its annual revenue was about twenty-five thousand dollars, half of which was due to the British as tribute.

After Karamchand Gandhi retired, he received a pension from the ruler of the Rajkot state, where he had been employed. Even if he had had the ambition to accumulate wealth, his chances would have been slim. But he was not money-minded and had no such goals. He acquired no property, so that the family had to live modestly, although still much better than most of the people.

Mother Putlibai was a saintly woman, a devoted follower of the Vaishnava sect, whose members venerated the god Vishnu. She could neither read nor write, but she liked to listen to the recital of ancient scripts, especially the *Ramayana,* the epic story of the noble Rama, who was deprived of his throne by court intrigues. She also enjoyed the *Upanishads,* which contain ethical principles, and which culminate in the confession of faith in truth: "Truth conquers everything, falsehood nothing"; and in the invocation: "Lead me to light from the darkness. From death lead me to immortality."

Mohandas Gandhi was only seven when a messenger arrived from Takur Sahib, head of the Rajkot state, some eighty miles northeast of Porbandar. The ruler asked Karamchand if he was ready to head the cabinet. The offer was accepted, and the entire family of six children and parents piled on top of a couple of oxcarts drawn by bullocks. It took three days to cover the eighty miles.

In the town of Rajkot, Mohandas became better acquainted with many problems of India. He became familiar with the "communal problem" of his native land, resulting from the existence of several large religions.

One day Mohandas noticed a great number of people going through what seemed to him strange physical exercises. He watched them crouching, then rising and throwing themselves on the ground. Next they stood up and, swaying their bodies, repeated certain words which Mohandas could not understand. He could hardly wait to ask his father.

"*Bapu* (father)," he said breathlessly, "I saw lots of

people crouching in a big courtyard. Who were they and what were they doing?"

"They were Muslims," his father answered, "and they were praying."

"Who are the Muslims? They don't pray like you and *ba*."

Bapu told him briefly about one of India's great problems—its religious diversity. From his father's explanation and from other sources, Mohandas gained a fairly clear picture of the "communal problem."

"You are a Hindu," his father told him. "You know that. You worship our Hindu gods. The Muslims don't. They worship only one god, whom they call Allah."

The child burst out indignantly, "That's awful! Don't they know that there are forty crores of gods?"

Karamchand had no time for a long explanation. Also, he was not quite sure if he knew the answer. But once Mohandas wanted to get to the bottom of a question, he usually found a way. And so he asked neighbors, teachers, and "wise men" about the Muslims, and from them he learned a great deal.

Muslims formed about one tenth of the population; most other Indians were Hindus like himself. The Muslims had been rulers of India before the British came. Their customs were different from those of other Indians. One god, Allah, was their only god. They did not venerate the *Upanishads* and the *Vedas*, as the Hindus did. They believed in the Koran, their most sacred book.

The "gymnastic exercise" that Mohandas saw in the courtyard was the Muslim way of worshiping Allah. They prostrated themselves, facing the holy city of Mecca in Arabia, where their religion had originated. The courtyard surrounded the *masjid*, the Muslim shrine. Inside the shrine were other worshipers. The masjid had a slim tower with a balcony near the top. The tower was the minaret, and the *muezzin*, or herald, called the faithful to worship there five times a day.

The Muslims, Mohandas was told, did not believe in most of the things in which the Hindus believed. They did not believe, for instance, in the transmigration of the soul. Nor did they venerate the cow. On the contrary, they ate the meat of cattle, but they considered the pig an unclean animal and never touched pork. Although they lived in villages with Hindus, they kept to themselves. From time to time a dispute would erupt between the two sects, and then blood would be shed. It was one of the maintasks of a prime minister to keep the two "communities" from feuding.

Mohandas noticed that unlike Hindu women, Muslim women wore veils and baggy skirts of ankle length. He gradually learned that Muslims behaved differently from Hindus when they became ill. A Muslim would consult the *hakeem*, learned in the medicine of the Arabs and Greeks. The Hindu, on the other hand, turned to the *vaid*, learned in the Vedic system of medicine, based upon the Hindus' most ancient writs.

18

Muslims were buried with their faces turned toward Mecca, while Hindus were cremated and their ashes immersed in a sacred stream. The Ganges River in India is considered the most sacred. A Muslim child was given a distinctively Muslim name, such as Mohammed Ali, while the Hindu child was often named for Hindu gods, such as Krishna. In the case of Mohandas Gandhi, *Mohan* is another name for Krishna, and *das* means "servant."

Mohandas followed his parents' commands in practicing Hinduism. Now that he had become aware of the differences between the two main creeds of his country, he wanted to learn more about his own religion. *Bapu* was not up to the task of acquainting his son with the tenets of Hinduism, but his position as prime minister helped him to find a teacher—a *guru*—who was not only a learned man but who also knew how to explain religion to a child. Khushwant was the teacher's name, and his impression on the boy was great.

The guru told Mohandas that the good deed—*karma*—formed the core of their creed, and that a person's deeds determined his place in future life. He explained that a person had certain duties, *dharma*, to his family and to his caste. His future in the next life depended upon the performance of these duties.

Khushwant reminded Mohandas that life, even at its best, was filled with suffering, and that life in India was particularly hard because the country had too many peo-

ple and too little food. The best of all fates for any creature was, therefore, *nirvana,* the total end, a final release
from pain. It might require many rebirths, however, before a person could reach nirvana.

Mohandas was told about the special merit that a
Hindu could acquire by being kind to the cow, the symbol of kindness and fertility and the image of useful
life. Khushwant told him that the cow should always be
the object of special respect. He recounted the story of
Punya Koti—Million Merits—a fabulous cow.

One day Punya Koti went into the forest to graze. A
tiger leaped out of the brush, ready to attack. Punya Koti
told the tiger that she was not yet ready to be eaten because she had to feed her calf. The tiger explained that
he was hungry, too, and that it was the cow's duty to
satisfy his hunger. While the cow saw his point, she asked
him to let her go back home for a short time to give her
calf its last feeding. The tiger agreed on the condition
that she give him her word of honor to return.

Hours passed and the cow still did not come back.
Angrily, the tiger decided never to trust a cow again.
Then, toward midnight, the cow appeared, apologizing
for being late. She had had to make arrangements for the
feeding of her calf. Now, however, she was ready to be
eaten. The honesty of the cow so shook the tiger that
he fell on his back and died.

Because the cow plays a central role in the Hindu
creed, Mohandas' guru went into great detail. He told

him that the god Krishna was also known as the Lord of the Cows, and those who were kind to this supreme symbol of life were promised a special heaven of their own. The cow was seldom referred to as an animal, but was called *Go Matha*—Cow the Mother—and should be shown the affection accorded to the human mother. To kill Cow the Mother was as deadly a sin as to murder a human. Only the bandit torments the cow in Indian tales. Whenever danger threatens a town, the Angel of Destruction pauses to save women, children, and cows.

These explanations made a great impression on Mohandas Gandhi. Many years later, when his fame had spread throughout the world, the protection of cows formed a central point in his creed.

The boy showed vivid interest in religion, and Rajkot was a good place to observe the followers of many creeds. Among the people he saw in the bazaar and in the alleyways were some who covered their mouths with cloth, and he asked his guru about them.

They were people who called themselves conquerors, Jains, he was told, because they tried to subdue their lowest instincts. They kept their mouths covered so that not even a gnat would suffer by being inhaled with the air. They killed no living creature, not even the vermin.

"But then their huts must be overrun by them," Mohandas said.

"No," answered Khushwant. "Their huts are clean because they are extremely clean people, and vermin flourish on filth. Cleanliness is not only their social but their religious duty. They eat no meat and refrain from consuming honey and drinking alcohol. Indeed, they eat little and are very healthy people. They help one another, and many of them are among our most prosperous countrymen."

There were also a few Parsis in Rajkot. These were followers of a sect which dressed differently than others. The men wore knee-length black coats, and tall hats, called *feta*; the women wore beltlike *kusti*, a sacred cord. Many of them were wealthy traders. They summarized their ethical principles in three words: *humata* (good thoughts); *hukhata* (good words); and *huvrashta* (good deeds). The Parsis prayed before the sacred fire in their *agyari*, or fire temples. Many centuries before, their ancestors in Persia were known as Zoroastrians, who worshiped the God of Light, Ahura Mazda.

The Parsis maintained a *dakhma*—Tower of Silence—in Rajkot. On the top of the tower they left their dead. They did not want the dead cremated, as did their Hindu neighbors, because the Parsis considered fire sacred, and not to be used for cremation. Instead, the dead bodies were to be consumed by vultures.

Young Gandhi respected all the religions which he encountered under the influence of his learned guru. However, there was one religion for which his teacher held no respect. This was Christianity. The guru's attitude may have been due to his resentment of the British, who were members of the Church of England. At any rate, young Gandhi was under the influence of this attitude for many years. But the time would come when he would change his mind on the subject.

The more Mohandas heard about the creeds of India the more he preferred Hinduism. It was difficult, of course, for him to find his way in its maze of religious rules, the essence of which he was trying to grasp. Then one day *bapu* asked him to get his copybook and write out the sentence: "Religion is Truth. God is Truth."

The boy wrote it down and thought little of it. But he did not forget.

"I did not understand this at the time and was not ready to ask the question: What is truth? But I was thinking of that sentence for years and now I think I know what it means. Truth is the innermost law of nature. In nature there is no ruse. It commands all living creatures to be true to themselves and to follow its precepts. Human beings can be true to themselves only if they are true to others, who are their own mirror images. If they are not true to others, they destroy parts of themselves. The laws of nature are manifestations of God—Truth."

The guru exerted such a good influence on Mohandas that he was never to forget him. On the other hand, the boy learned little from his teachers at school. Several of them knew little themselves. They were half-starved individuals whose main task was to keep their unruly pupils from getting in one another's hair.

Mohandas Gandhi was a soft-spoken boy with a high-pitched voice. He was also a shy boy, who hardly dared to open his mouth in the presence of strangers. His timidity is noteworthy because the time was to come when his voice would be heard in all lands. Actually, his shyness may have been caused by the circumstances of his family life. His father was a man of commanding presence and great self-confidence. Karamchand Gandhi might have had good reason to be shy, because he was barely literate. But he made up in self-confidence what he lacked in literacy. He had the capacity to convince people that he was right, and—more important—to convince himself.

Young Mohandas was so awed by his impressive father that he hardly dared to talk. And the more quiet he became, the more the inner strength of *bapu* overwhelmed him. In turn, the "high-tension" father was irritated by his "low-tension" son. Yet, Mohandas loved his father. And above all he respected him as the confidant of princes and as a noted statesman.

2

Marriage and a Trip

Mohandas Gandhi was five years old when he became
engaged to be married. His first intended bride was a
child who died. A year later he was again engaged, and
again the girl died. In India marriages were contracted
at a very early age—sometimes even before the age of five.
By the time children reached fifteen, four out of five were
married.

It was not easy to find a suitable mate for Mohandas,
and his parents did a great deal of searching. The prospective bride had to come from the same caste and subcaste. Also, the parents of the girl had to be wealthy
enough to afford costly wedding rites. The children
should speak the same language and preferably the same
dialect; this in itself was difficult since there are hundreds
of dialects in India. Their skin coloring should be
matched, too. Light-skinned parents wanted light-skinned

in-laws. Also, a proper time had to be selected for the wedding.

Mohandas was seven years old when he was again engaged to be married. His fiancée was as old as he, and her name was Kasturbai, the daughter of Gokuldas Makanji. Her father belonged to the Bania subcaste of the Vaisya caste, the same as the Gandhis. He was a well-to-do merchant, and could pay his share of the wedding. Kasturbai's native language was Gujarati. Also, there was little difference in the coloring of the children's skins. Merchant Makanji was a devotee of the Vaishnava sect, attending the same shrine as the Gandhis.

The prospective bride and groom were brought together. Too young to know what marriage meant, first they were to become acquainted with one another in play. In a few years they would be husband and wife.

Meanwhile Mohandas finished his elementary education and was enrolled in the high school of Rajkot. The language of instruction for some of his courses was now English. Until this time he had mastered only his native Gujarati. Young Mohandas was still a spindly-legged youth, with narrow shoulders and protruding ears, his owl-like dark eyes blinking with embarrassment in the presence of elders. As the years advanced, he became even more shy than before. He was often the target of bullies whom he could not fight, because he was not their equal in strength and because fighting was not in his nature.

His prospective bride did not go to school, since it was not considered essential for girls to be educated. In her father's house, she attended to household chores, preparatory to marriage. Because Mohandas looked so young and weak, it was decided not to rush into the marriage but to wait until he had reached an older age.

When Mohandas became thirteen, his parents decided to go ahead with the wedding. It was indeed a complex matter. A wedding was the best way in India to show that one could keep up with his neighbor. The parents in both households were ready to bankrupt themselves for the sake of one big affair. In this case, it was not only one wedding but four in one, since Mohandas' elder brothers and a cousin were to be married at the same time.

The prospective spouses were not informed about the time of the marriages since it was not considered their business. But Mohandas and his bride got an inkling of it when their parents presented them with new clothes.

The wedding was to take place in the Gandhis' ancestral town of Porbandar. This time the journey took five days to cover one hundred and twenty miles. Father Gandhi was in a great hurry to reach his destination ahead of the others, and he was allowed to use the prince's stagecoach. The coach was good but the road was bad, and so there was an accident. Portly Karamchand Gandhi spilled out of the coach, trying to break the record of five miles per hour. He was badly bruised, and a couple of bones were broken. But the marriage ceremony could not be delayed.

The festive moment finally approached. There was much beating of drums to scare away unfriendly spirits. The children were given a paste with which to smear their bodies. This would attract friendly spirits. The most solemn part of the ceremony began when Mohandas and Kasturbai mounted the dais. Ancient rituals had to be performed so that the married life of the young ones would be happy. First came the ceremony of the *sapta-padi,* or seven steps. As the entire audience observed in hushed silence, the children arose slowly and took seven steps while exchanging the sacred formula of marriage vows. The steps completed, they were linked to each other for life. The vows were sealed when the wedded children placed sweet *kansar*—wheat mash—in each other's mouths. This had a ritual meaning, indicating that they were to nurture each other throughout their lives.

To the newly married couple, the ceremony was "fun." Years later, Gandhi looked upon early weddings with disapproval. Parents should not make such a choice for their children, he believed. While it was traditional to marry early, he felt that it was wrong to have children wedded at the age of thirteen or fourteen. Both he and his wife, he said, were not sufficiently mature to realize the significance of the "seven steps." However, Gandhi and Kasturbai were to have a long and happy life together.

Marriage and a Trip

Even though he was now a married man, Gandhi continued his studies. His record as a student was not impressive. He could not cope with the problems of mathematics. However, one day one of his teachers devoted extra time to initiate him into the key propositions of Euclid, the "father of mathematics." Thenceforth, Gandhi's attitude toward mathematics changed, and he found the subject fascinating.

He had trouble with languages, too, since in the higher grades his teachers used English, in which textbooks were more readily available. On a still higher level, students had the choice of either Sanskrit or Persian as a third language. Gandhi selected Persian, which seemed easier to him since it had been the common language of much of India. Later he regretted that his choice had not been Sanskrit, the language of the Hindus' sacred writs.

In later life Gandhi reached the conclusion that Indians should study half a dozen languages. Besides their own native tongue and English, he felt that they should learn Sanskrit, Hindi, and Arabic: Hindi because more people in India speak it than any other tongue; Arabic because it is the language of the Indian Muslims' sacred book.

Marriage did not improve Mohandas' record as a scholar. When sitting in the classroom his mind was more often on his wife than on his studies. Later in life he blamed child marriages for having kept him and his schoolmates from giving their best to their studies.

Some of his married schoolmates—often barely ten years old—were even less effective in their classroom work than he, and the masters sometimes applied the switch. It was not unusual for the husbands to rush home after class and sobbingly tell their wives that they had been spanked.

Physical exercise was one of the required subjects in school. Gandhi disliked it, probably because he was conscious of his spindly legs and narrow chest. He was impressed by the boys who distinguished themselves in such team sports as cricket and soccer, which the British had introduced into India.

Mohandas preferred physical exercise of another sort, which he could do alone. He liked to take long walks, in and out of town, in the bazaars and open fields, observing the lush landscape of his native land. He liked to walk at night under the deep blue canopy of the sky. When walking, Mohandas never felt that he was alone. Instead, he felt the presence of an all-pervading force, one supreme manifestation of the countless gods of India, keeping close watch over him.

The young boy strictly observed the rules of his religion. Members of his caste were vegetarians, who refrained from eating animal products, including eggs and milk. Violating these religious laws would have been an enormous sin to the boy brought up in the Hindu orthodox belief.

Then one day Mohandas learned that not all Hindu boys shared his beliefs. There were those who had formed a secret society among themselves, preparing to violate religious law by eating meat. They had decided to do this out of a sense of patriotic obligation. They had reached their decision in the following way.

They knew that a handful of Britishers ruled over hundreds of millions of Indians. Investigating the cause of this fact, they decided that the eating habits of the two peoples were at the heart of the problem. The British rulers were strong because they ate meat. The Indian masses, on the other hand, did not eat meat, and therefore were weak. To become strong, the boys believed, the Indians must eat meat. They would then acquire the strength to overwhelm the British masters and regain their own country.

The boys sang this song:

> *Behold the mighty Englishman*
> *He rules the Indian small,*
> *Because being a meat-eater,*
> *He is five cubits tall.*

Mohandas was admitted into this secret society. Until then he had not paid too much attention to the plight of India. He assumed, as did most of his friends, that the gods had ruled that this should be the condition of his people. He personally had no cause to complain against the Englishmen, because of his father's high position.

Members of the secret society explained to Mohandas that an Indian head of state had only those rights that the British allowed, and even this system could be changed overnight if the British so desired. Also, they told him that a much larger portion of the Indian people were directly under English rule, and that the native princes had nothing to say in those areas. The boys recounted the glorious past of India, contrasting it dramatically with the poverty-stricken present. They reminded Mohandas that people from all over the world at one time had tried to find the way to India—the Promised Land—filled with all the treasures people coveted: precious stones, gold, perfumes, and expensive spices. In those days Indians were clad in silk. Now they covered their bodies with rags. And why this contrast? Because of British rule. And how could it be changed? By eating meat.

Mohandas was an impressionable youth, who could easily be persuaded to have a hand in the "plot." He told his fellow conspirators, however, that never would he eat any part of a cow. He was assured that he would not be asked to do that. Instead, he would be given goat's meat. Then Mohandas told them that they must select a spot to eat meat where the gods would not see them. It should be on the bank of the river Aji, hidden behind thick clumps of bushes. The boys agreed.

The great day came. They met on the riverbank behind the trees. One of them took a piece of goat's meat
from a bag. It was badly cooked and had a foul taste.
Mohandas chewed only a morsel and became violently
sick. As if chased by evil spirits, he dashed home and
went to bed. He felt miserable and developed a fever.
During the night he had a nightmare: The goat that he
had tasted started to bleat piteously in his stomach.

In spite of this bad start, Mohandas was challenged
to continue the experiment. His fellow "plotters" found
a new way to impress him. They told him that eating
meat would straighten his legs and make him strong.
They admitted that the meat they had eaten was leathery,
but now they brought pieces of pork, which tasted good.

The boys turned the eating of meat into a ritual, a
patriotic obligation, and they kept it up for over a year.
Mohandas watched his legs and chest month after month.
Were they getting stronger? He saw no change. Nor did
he notice that the others were growing as tall as the Britishers. Suddenly he was gripped by a strong feeling of
remorse, realizing that he had violated the commands of
his creed. He decided to make a clean breast of his "sin,"
but he hesitated at the last moment. His father was old,
and Mohandas feared that the shock might endanger his
health. Still, Mohandas decided to put an end to his
participation in the "plot." By the temple of Vishnu,
he made a vow never again to touch meat. He was never
to forget this vow, which he considered not only a re-

ligious obligation but a matter of personal honor, and so he remained faithful to it all his life.

Another crisis now entered the life of the boy. His father had developed a skin disease on his leg, which demanded daily attention. Local people tried to cure it with household herbs, invoking the aid of local gods. Yet the condition grew worse. An official of the princely court recommended that a noted British surgeon be consulted, and this was done. The Englishman advised surgery, which the family council, influenced by the family local "doctor," immediately rejected.

Every day the patient's condition deteriorated. The disease spread to the other leg, then to the entire body. Now it was too late to perform surgery. The family merely tried to ease the pain. Two family members were in constant attendance—a brother of the sick man and his son Mohandas.

One day the elder Gandhi's condition was particularly bad. His brother came to relieve Mohandas, who went to his wife. He felt uneasy about leaving his father's bedside, but he comforted himself with the thought that it was now his uncle's turn to attend to the sick man's needs.

Mohandas had been with his wife for only five minutes when a loud knock on the door startled him. He did not want to be disturbed, and he asked in an irritated tone, "What do you want?"

"Come quickly, master, *bapu* is very sick."

34

Reluctant to leave, Mohandas said, "I saw him only five minutes ago."

At this the servant broke into a loud wail, and Mohandas sensed what it meant. He rushed to the door of the sickroom and found his uncle closing the eyes of the dead man.

This was another incident which Gandhi was never to forget. Nor was he ever to forgive himself for not rushing to his father's bedside as soon as he was called. Now it was too late to tell his father about eating meat, and therefore it was too late to hope for forgiveness for his sin.

The year of his father's death was 1886, and Mohandas was seventeen years old. So great was the shock he experienced that he responded to it in an impulsive way. Always religious (despite eating the forbidden meat, which he called "The Tragedy" all his life), he now became a religious devotee. Every day he frequented the Vaishnava shrines, and imposed many religious obligations upon himself. He wondered which of the many gods could provide solace and show him the way. Should it be Krishna? His own name meant servant of that god. Yes, he was devoted to Lord Krishna with all his heart, trying to follow his teachings, the most important of which was to overcome base instincts. It surely must have been a base instinct that had lured him from his father's sickbed. This thought kept haunting him.

Another Hindu god appealed to Mohandas with spe-

35

cial force. It was this god whose words he would seek to heed all his life, whose names he would invoke in times of trial, and whom he would call to many years later when he himself was about to die. The god was Rama, one of the incarnations of Vishnu. To Mohandas Gandhi, Rama represented divine, all-embracing providence—truthful, and ready to help. He was also the "intelligence" moving the world, the mysterious system that kept the heavenly bodies on their appointed courses. In years to come, when these words meant even more to Mohandas Gandhi, he summed up his creed in this way: "Utter the name of Rama with every word you breathe."

"Follow divine principles in all your actions," he would later urge the people of India.

In his sorrow, young Gandhi began to understand the meaning of a famous Gujarati stanza:

> *For a bowl of water give a goodly meal,*
> *For a kindly greeting bow down with great zeal,*
> *For a single penny pay thou back with gold*
> *If thy life be rescued, life do not withhold;*
> *Thus the words and actions of the wise regard,*
> *Every little service tenfold they reward,*
> *But the truly noble know all men as one,*
> *And return with gladness good for evil done.*

Now that *bapu* was dead, what was Mohandas to do? He had to acquire a higher education; it was the wish of the family. Although his father had held a high rank, he had never accumulated wealth. Mohandas had to think of the future; how was he to support Kasturbai, himself, and the children they would have?

Higher education could not be had in his native town. He would have to go to the city of Ahmadabad, with a population of half a million at that time. Its Gujarat College had a good reputation in the entire Northern Division of Bombay, of which it was a part. Ahmadabad had everything a young scholar needed, particularly books and newspapers not available at home. Also, it had history, represented in beautiful buildings combining the architecture of the Hindus with that of the Arabs, who had spread their creed to large portions of the Indian population.

Mohandas went to Ahmadabad and took the college entrance test. Although he passed it, he abandoned his plan to settle there. It was too far from his home, from his caste, and from his family. He would have been a total stranger in the city. Instead, Mohandas decided to continue his studies in an environment where his family was known and respected. Therefore he entered Samaldas College in the state of Baunager. It was located on the Gulf of Cambay, facing the Arabian Sea. Its small harbor attracted vessels from other parts of India. Young Gandhi seemed to prefer places from which he would have a broad view of the outside world.

Gandhi's stay at Samaldas College did not last long.

Probably he was not sufficiently interested in the subjects he had to take. And he had not yet overcome his shyness. Afraid to face his teachers, he could not hold his own in tests. He was easily rattled, forgetting his lessons and becoming confused. Indeed, Mohandas gave the impression of one who was not likely to hold down even an average job. He remained at the school for only one semester and then dropped out. Now what was to become of the son of the late Prime Minister Karamchand Gandhi?

The question had to be answered soon enough. And it had to be answered even sooner when his wife presented him with a sturdy son. The child, born in 1888, was dedicated to the god Shiva, one of the three major gods of the creed. Shiva was also called Hari, and the boy was given the name of Harilal, son of Shiva, the firstborn.

Nineteen years was considered a mature age in India, and so it was not unusual that Mohandas Gandhi should become a father at that time. But now it was really urgent that he be able to support his family.

Besides his mother and Mohandas himself, other kinsfolk and friends of the family were concerned about his future. One of his friends, Mavji Davi, affectionately called Joshiji, had the honor of suggesting a career that was to change the life of Mohandas Gandhi—and also of India. He spoke about it to *ba*.

Normally Joshiji's booming voice would shake the rafters, but this time he talked in whispers, and yet loud enough so that Mohandas heard him in the next room.

"I have been thinking of your son," Joshiji began. "He dropped out of Samaldas; I know that. He is extremely shy; I know that, too. Yet—I have a strange feeling about him. He has something inside which he has not been able to reveal so far. Character; let's call it that. Yes, it is character, and also honesty. He has not found his right environment, I believe, since he has never been exposed to real challenge. He should be exposed to it."

Putlibai tried to interrupt him, but Joshiji was not a man to be stopped.

"Wait, I have not finished," he said. "Suppose he were pushed to complete his studies in a provincial college. What would he become? An attorney. He was headed in that direction. The competition in that field is fierce and he is a shy young man. I have another idea for him— it may shock you—please don't interrupt me."

This introduction alone was enough to frighten Putlibai into silence.

"You must possess something different in these days of competition, so that you can stand out in the crowd. In this part of India we have our own princes, and therefore we cherish the impression that this is our own country. It is not. Even in our princely states it is the British who run our show. Our system of laws is complicated. Increasingly, British law influences our lives. You must be familiar with their legal system if you want to plead a case in higher courts. And also you must be familiar with their ways if you want to break into politics. You can see that a young man who wishes to get ahead must study in England."

This suggestion made Putlibai gasp.

"You don't mean to say that—"

This time it was Joshiji who interrupted.

"I warned you not to be shocked, and I mean precisely that. I mean that he should go abroad for his studies. Just like you, I am a Bania, and perfectly familiar with our caste obligations. Some of them are good, others are antiquated. Our caste rules forbid the crossing of the seas, and Mohandas would have to do that. Why not cross the seas? So as not to be contaminated abroad, our regulations say. Contaminated? Where is it that people die of the plague? Certainly not in London. Yet they die like flies in India. It is against our caste rules, too, to wear European garments. In the English climate he would die if he were to wear our flimsy clothes. He would have to read in English and not in Gujarati. I assume that London has no shrine of the Vaishnava sect. But then you know that real religion is not always in the temples but in the human heart.

"Your husband's family was that of dewans: cabinet members and even prime ministers. Mohandas should try to follow in their footsteps. With his present preparation, he would qualify only as a scribbler for a prince. If he studies in Britain, where the competition would force him to shed his shyness, and then he returns to us, he will be at the head of the pack, an eminent barrister or, if he wants it, even a dewan."

After this long speech, Joshiji took a breath, prepared to be overwhelmed by Putlibai's reproaches. But she remained speechless. Yet thoughts filled her mind.

To Gandhi's mother, Britain was a blurred image at the other end of the world. It was an alien land in which people were constantly violating the laws of the Bania caste. Her stomach turned at the very thought that the British ate meat, and cow meat at that. She had been told that people had to eat meat in Britain in order to endure the climate. They drank liquor, too, to dull their senses against cruelties of nature that denied them the warming sun. Besides, at the age of nineteen, Mohandas had been a family man for many years; he was the father of a son. He was too old now to engage in studies which would take years. And suppose even these handicaps could be removed—who would cover the enormous costs? And if someone did, would Mohandas drop out of college again? She would not be able to survive the shame.

Joshiji conceded that the costs were high, but he said that an important cause demanded great sacrifices. Even though Putlibai knew that his suggestion was motivated by the best intentions, she decided to take a stand against it. She called Mohandas, in the belief that, shy as he was, he would recoil with horror from the thought of leaving his home.

But her son surprised her.

"Yes, the competition at school was fierce but—" At that point, he appeared to be a new man. "In England

I would get a head start over all the others," he said. "What are you afraid of, *ba*, if we are able to get the funds?"

His mother poured out her fears to him. Death held no terrors for her, a devoted follower of the Vaishnava, but she was worried about what would happen to Mohandas after his death. If he broke the sacred laws of his caste, he might become a loathsome insect when he ended his present tour in this world.

Putlibai could not recognize her son in his sudden new role. He seemed to be bursting with energy. He wanted to sail to England, beyond the unfathomable seas. He wanted to see the land that produced the mighty Englishmen, so healthy and superior.

Mohandas spoke with finality. "*Ba*, before I cross the seas, I'll solicit the permission of my caste brothers. As to your other fears, let me now take a solemn vow: No matter what the temptation, I'll never eat meat nor taste alcohol. The cost of a stay in England for my family would be prohibitive, of course, and so I would have to go alone. But—and this is part of my vow—I'll remain faithful to Kasturbai, as I have been to this day."

Ba still looked for a way out. She said that she must consult a family friend, a holy monk in the strict Jain sect, Becharji Swami, and his decision would be final. She thought that the holy man would take her side. But he did not.

"I shall have Mohandas repeat his solemn vow to me,"

the monk told Putlibai, "and then you may let him go."

Putlibai had to resign herself. But one question still needed an answer: Where was the money to come from? In finding it, Mohandas developed a character trait that swept all opposition out of the way. He approached the head of his clan—an uncle—and also an elder brother. They had the money to pay for the overseas trip, and he convinced them to let him sail.

The greatest obstacle was still to be overcome: the permission of the caste to cross the seas. To get that permission, Mohandas had to go to Bombay, the gateway of India. A general assembly of the Modh-Bania subcaste was quickly called to decide his fate, and to it Mohandas presented his appeal. The answer of the subcaste's headman allowed no contradiction. He said that no member of the subcaste had ever taken a boat to cross the seas. Also, the caste would not allow any of its members to share the Englishmen's "disgusting habit" of eating meat.

Working himself into a frenzy, the headman asked, "Do you want to be like an Englishman?"

Gandhi informed the gathering that he had the approval of a Brahman, of a holy man, and of his *ba*. He had not only the approval of his uncle and of his elder brother, but also their financial aid. However, no argument made a dent in the assembly's determination to deny him permission to leave. As members of the caste approached Mohandas to reinforce the headman's words with their personal appeals, the meeting became unruly.

But Gandhi remained adamant. There was now only one more step that the headman could take, and he used it. He pronounced the dreaded words that severed the boy from his caste, which was also his religion.

"Unless he repents and abandons his monstrous plan," the headman intoned, "this boy shall be treated as an outcaste."

Years later, when he became world famous, his caste was delighted to have him in its ranks.

Gandhi did not abandon his plan. On the contrary, more than ever he wanted to go. Yet he was determined to observe every syllable of his solemn vow to *ba*.

From Bombay, on a hot and humid September day in 1888, Gandhi took a ship of the Peninsular and Oriental line. This was a new experience for him, and the vastness of the Indian Ocean awed him. He was pleased to set eyes on Aden, a British outpost in the Middle East.

The ship sailed up the Red Sea, where it was even hotter than in India. Moving very slowly, it sailed through the Suez Canal, and at the northern end, in Port Said, the British flag waved proudly. The boat reached the Mediterranean, and its next stop was Malta, another pivot along Britain's globe-encircling lifeline. Mohandas enjoyed the trip in the enchanted world of caressing sun and azure sea. After a time the ship reached Britain's proudest possession, Gibraltar. For weeks the British vessel had been plowing the waters of many seas, and everywhere Mohandas was confronted with England's might.

Determined not to eat meat, Mohandas had a supply of vegetables and fruits which he had brought from home. He had been warned that because of the climate he would have to eat meat once past Gibraltar. But he remained steadfast to his vow.

An elderly Englishman took a liking to the shy boy from India, inquiring about his home and telling him of Britain's ways. Mohandas Gandhi, thinking of his vow to his mother, asked the Englishman to sign a certificate attesting to the fact that he had not touched meat or alcohol. The friendly Britisher signed it promptly, and this very act made Mohandas wonder. How could the Englishman know that the young Indian had not eaten the forbidden food? Mohandas reached the conclusion that certificates of compliance with caste rules were worth little. Never again did he ask anybody to sign such a certificate.

After Gibraltar, the scene and the climate changed. They were now in the churning waters of the Atlantic Ocean. As they proceeded northward, the wind took on a cutting edge. Day after day, the rain chased Mohandas belowdecks.

It was on a Sunday in October that young Gandhi set foot on the soil of England, the land which was to play a great role in his life. The people who saw him descending the gangplank could not have suspected that they were seeing a man who was to become a historic figure.

In England, Gandhi wanted to look like a Britisher. He had seen Englishmen in India wearing white flannels, and he had brought a pair with him, which he put on before landing. So on a cold and rainy English day, Mohandas Gandhi walked down the gangplank in his tropical suit.

3

England and Its Aftermath

Young Gandhi threw himself into his work with considerable zest. He wanted to justify the faith and expenses of his kinsmen. Also, he wanted to live frugally, to be less of a financial burden on his people at home. He found a room in the West Kensington section of London, in the house of a widow. He studied common law—the pivot of the legal system of England—at University College, and found it more to his liking than his previous studies in India. Common law, he discovered, was "common sense."

Still a naïve young man, Gandhi took seriously the advice given to him—probably with tongue in cheek—that an English gentleman must be accomplished in French, dancing, and elocution. He studied French, but did not get very far with it, for he was not gifted as a linguist.

47

He took dancing lessons, but he had no rhythm. He decided to sharpen his sense of rhythm by taking violin lessons but got nowhere with that, either. He also took elocution lessons, but that, too, did not turn out to be a success. Because of his failures he felt gloomy about his future career. Was it to be his fate always to remain average? How could he justify the aid he had received from his relatives?

There was always a mystic trait in Mohandas Gandhi, particularly when he felt trapped. On such occasions he turned to religion. An English friend interested him in Christianity. He read the Bible but showed little enthusiasm for it until he read the Sermon on the Mount. Its sweep of grand thoughts and profound human sympathies carried him away and he learned its words by heart.

"But I say unto ye, Resist not evil: but whosoever shall smite thee on the right cheek, turn to him the other also. And if any man will sue thee at the law, and take away thy coat, let him have thy cloak also."

"How did you like it?" his English friend asked.

"Very much," he said. "Very much indeed."

Although Gandhi was a Hindu, his religion did not instruct him to avoid the sacred books of other creeds. The Sermon on the Mount did, indeed, make an overwhelming impression on the young man from India. That impression became a conviction, which, in turn, grew into an abiding belief, and the belief was transformed into a mode of life. The time was to come when the young man's way of life would be the official policy of a great political party in India, and the party would become the pivot of a peoples' struggle for freedom and independence. The teaching of the Sermon on the Mount was a foundation for the basic thought of what was to become the Gandhian creed.

The language of the Sermon, too, made a deep impression on Gandhi. It was forthright, without embellishment, and yet beautiful, motivated by the noblest of impulses. Gandhi was never to forget that language. The time came when all of India—and later all of the world—listened to his words. On those occasions, he used the language style of the Sermon on the Mount.

In the course of his law studies, Gandhi's readings encompassed a large field of the humanities. He was swayed by the writings that stimulate man to shed the animal in himself and to turn to efforts that would reveal the Godlike spark in him. It was in search of such words that Gandhi encountered the writings of an American author who was to exercise a dominant influence on his thoughts. The author was Henry David Thoreau.

Thoreau believed that human dignity was not merely an empty phrase but a regulation of human conduct. He held that no man had the right to consider himself superior to another, because such feelings inevitably led to oppression. In line with his humanitarian thoughts, Thoreau considered the institution of slavery in America humiliating, not only for slave but also for master. He made up his mind that as long as slavery was protected by the government, he would not pay taxes. Eventually his refusal to pay landed him in jail. In the light of such experiences, Thoreau wrote these famous lines in his publication on civil disobedience.

"If the law is of such a nature that it requires you to be an agent of injustice to another, then I say, break the law."

Mohandas Gandhi was particularly impressed by these words. As a young man from India, his impressions meant little for the world at the time. But he was to remember them in years to come, providing him with the guiding line that led to Gandhism.

The Sermon on the Mount and the teachings of Thoreau did not remain alone in Gandhi's mind. At home he had been an avid reader of the *Bhagavad Gita*, and the words of that famous poem of Sanskrit literature acquired fresh meaning for him when related to his newly gained insights. His readings of the Bible, of the American author, and of the *Gita* showed him the path to a new goal. But the question now arose: Who was worthy of taking that path? The answer was provided by the sacred Hindu writ:

"If one ponders on the objects of the sense, there springs attraction; from which there grows desire; and from it flames fierce passion; which breeds recklessness. Then the memory—all betrayed—lets noble purpose go, saps the mind, until purpose, mind, and man are all undone."

Here was a warning that noble decisions and acts were accessible only to those who approached them with pure hearts. Gandhi made the vow that he would be one of them. At the time he did not know that he would be the greatest of them all.

Through his reading, West and East became fused in his mind, inspiring him to a noble quest of noble truths. But Gandhi was a son of India and the son of Putlibai, to whom he had given his solemn vow to abide by the instructions of his creed.

He remained a son of India by refusing to touch meat and drink alcohol. He lived on vegetables and fruits. After a while he realized that the food he ate was not sufficiently nourishing to keep him fit for his studies. Were those friends right who had warned him that in Britain people had to eat meat or else they died? He was not quite sure. Yet he was determined never to touch meat. How was he going to live?

One day when wandering in the chill air of London, he wondered about his fate. At home he had seen people dying of starvation. Not his type of people, of course, not members of the better classes. Would it not be strange if he were to die of starvation in England, the land of the well-fed people?

Then Gandhi saw a sign above a store which said "Vegetarian Restaurant." He had never heard of such a place in London. He entered the restaurant, sat down at a table which was neatly covered with a white cloth, and looked around. The people he saw were not famished

Indians, but Englishmen—plump, rosy-cheeked, bursting with health. Yet, they were vegetarians; they ate no meat. Gandhi ordered food, and it was good. He filled his empty stomach, and he was filled with a glow. There was no need for him to starve in London.

He found other vegetarian restaurants, too, frequented by healthy-looking people. In some of them he noticed periodicals for vegetarians. He also found books about vegetarianism. He read the views of well-informed writers that vegetarians were likely to enjoy better health than meat eaters, and thus live longer.

Gandhi was motivated to take a step which he would not have dared to take in India. He decided to call on the editor of one of the vegetarian publications. After all, he reflected, he came from a country in which people did not eat meat as a religious obligation, and the editor might be interested in the ways of hundreds of millions of vegetarians.

The British editor was encouraging. Englishmen knew little, he told Gandhi, about the Indians' attitude toward the cow and about the basic causes of their vegetarianism. Then, he added that what the English knew about these things might not be correct anyway. He asked Gandhi to write an article concerning the role of the cow in Hinduism.

The night after this visit, Mohandas Gandhi tossed on his bed sleeplessly. He could not get over his luck about the prospect of having an article printed in England. He wrote on "Cow Protection In India," and submitted it to the editor. The editor read it, liked it, and said he would print it. Gandhi would be paid a small fee.

After hearing this news, Gandhi could sleep even less than before. He was going to see his by-line—"by Mohandas Gandhi." How would his words look on the printed page? He had never had such an experience. Would people like his article? What about his mother and his other kinsfolk? Would they be proud of him? The article would be additional proof that he had kept his oath and touched no meat.

Copies of the periodical were available on the newsstands on a Tuesday. On the day that his article was to appear, Gandhi was up before dawn, trying to restrain his excitement. He passed the newsstand once, then again. The magazine was not there. He became panicky. It may have stopped publication; there may have been a strike; the editor may have succumbed to a heart attack. He continued on his rounds, then came back again. The news vendor looked at him suspiciously. What did this darkskinned creature want? He decided to keep Gandhi under observation. But it was not necessary. The next time Mohandas came around, the magazine was on the stand. Young Gandhi bought it, opened it with fevered haste, and there was his article in all its glory. There was his by-line, too. Never had he seen such a beautiful sight.

This was the beginning of an extended period of collaboration. Gandhi wrote a series of articles. What he wrote must have seemed strange to Englishmen, even if they were vegetarians, because of the Indians' attitude toward meat, and especially the cow. Gandhi hoped to convince the English that when the Indian spoke about the cow he did not mean merely an animal but a venerated symbol of life.

"The cow is the personification of innocence," Gandhi wrote. "Cow protection is one of the most wonderful phenomena of human evolution. It takes the human being beyond his species. Man through the cow is the best companion, the giver of plenty. Not only does she give milk but she also makes farming possible. The cow is a poem of pity, too. She is the mother of millions of Indian mankind. Protection of the cow means protection of all of the whole dumb creation of God."

And what about cow protection? Gandhi advocated the retirement of cows into forest tracts, and he proved with figures that his country was large enough to provide pasture for all of its retired cows. He also advocated better organization for improving the lot of the cow through cooperative ownership.

He examined in detail the whole range of the problem of the cow, from its calf stage to its death and to the utilization of its skin.

"There is at present a close race for life being run between the cow and the man of India. And if the cow is not scientifically bred and profitably used, she must eat us or be eaten by us."

He explained the religious aspect of the problem. The

Vedas, ancient scriptures on which Hinduism is based, placed the cow very high. They said that there was a celestial cow, Kamadhenu, the ancestor of all cows. While having the body of the cow, Kamadhenu had the face of a lovely woman. Indian mythology speaks of a great battle between a king with a mighty army and an unarmed sage who owned Kamadhenu and would not surrender her to the king. At the crucial moment, Kamadhenu produced an army by magic to aid the sage.

Time passed quickly for Gandhi as he studied law, read books, and wrote for the magazine. He was doing well in his studies as the time approached when they would end. He was admitted to the bar on June 10, 1891, and the following day was enrolled in the High Court. However, he could not afford to waste another day, and so, on June 12, he boarded a P. & O. steamer for Bombay. He did not want to be a burden to his family. It was his plan to make his living as an attorney and repay his kin.

On the way home Gandhi had time to think about the future. The air was hot when he reached the Arabian Sea, and it almost stifled him at the majestic Indian gateway of Bombay.

Gandhi's brother met him on the pier, looking downcast. The sea voyage had taken weeks, and Gandhi had received no letters from his family for some time. He looked into his brother's face and sensed what had happened.

"*Ba?*" The word leapt from his mouth.

55

His brother's slender frame was convulsed with sobs. "Yes," he answered.

Putlibai had been fifty years old when she died while Gandhi was on the high seas. In India, fifty years was twenty more than the average span of life.

Ba Putlibai had often been in Gandhi's thoughts during his stay in England. He wanted to justify her faith in him. Recalling the shattering news of her death, Gandhi remarked: "Most of my cherished hopes were shattered. My grief was even greater than over my father's death."

But the young man could not afford to be downed by his grief. He was a family man with a wife and three-year-old son to support. Now that he had a London diploma, he hoped to be able to make a living. Where would he practice law? Not in Porbandar, for although he was attached to the place of his birth, it was too small. Bombay was the logical place to launch a career. There he had his best chance to represent tradesmen, bankers, and other affluent people. But even now that Gandhi had his diploma, he was still strangely lacking in self-confidence. Least of all did he have the confidence in himself to convince potential clients that he was competent to work on their behalf.

Gandhi was also dismayed to find that even though he had a London law degree, he still lacked the experience to handle cases in Bombay. India had an infinitely complicated system of laws, because it was a tremendously

56

complicated country where layers upon layers of law systems had to be mastered. This was because all the conquerors who had overwhelmed the peninsula had brought their own law systems with them and had deposited them in a veritable legal jungle.

Further complications were caused by the influence of the dominant religions. The Hindus had traditional laws that were more ethical principles than specific rules. The Muslims had traditions; and so did the Jains, the Parsis, the Christians, and the other creeds. ·

There were the laws and ordinances, valid only in the India of the more than five hundred princes. It was all a vast maze of impenetrable systems, again complicated by the hairsplitting practices of generations of attorneys. There were also the laws and ordinances passed by the British in the part of the country which they ruled directly.

Being a conscientious young man, Gandhi was not the attorney to rush into this thicket of legal systems, trusting to good luck that he would find his way in the maze. Years were needed, he felt, before he would dare to trust his knowledge. Yet, there was no time to wait. He must repay his loans and support his family.

Where did a lawyer of twenty-two, with a brand new shingle, get his first cases? And why should clients go to him instead of to experienced barristers? Gandhi did not know the answers. Consequently, the "reception room" of his small law office was empty. Barristers had to have contacts, and so members of his family tried to help. But Gandhi's shyness scared away most of his prospective clients.

At last a small case came his way, to be tried in the Small Causes Court. For a long time Gandhi studied the case, which did not seem to be particularly complicated. On the day of the trial, he entered the courtroom, bathed in sweat which did not come from the heat. Young Gandhi represented the defendant. In the course of the trial, it became his turn to cross-examine the plaintiff. He was full of questions, but he did not know which to ask first, and so he did not cross-examine the plaintiff at all. He became completely tongue-tied and paralyzed with an unnamed fear. The judge, surprised and sympathetic, tried to help him, but it was no use. This was a day of shame for the young barrister, and the case was transferred to a more experienced lawyer.

What was he to do now? He may have been intimidated by Bombay—too big a place, its people too shrewd. Perhaps he should return to Rajkot where his name was familiar because of his father's fame. Consequently he and his family moved back to that small princely capital. This time Gandhi did not trust himself with another court case. He undertook merely the functions of a solicitor, drawing up briefs and preparing the trials conducted by the barristers.

In this way Gandhi made a modest living, aided by family contacts. A year after his return home, his second son, Manilal, was born. This increased both his responsibilities and the need for a more adequate income. He realized that because of his shyness he had no hope of following in Karamchand's footsteps; he could not become a dewan in a princely court. A London law degree alone was not sufficient for that. His father, without a degree, had possessed the self-confidence which Gandhi lacked.

This seemed the end of the road for Mohandas Gandhi at the age of twenty-three. Yet, at the very time that he was plunged into despondency, he received an offer to try his luck overseas. The offer, transmitted to him through one of his kinsmen, was for a temporary job, and not a very enticing one at that.

There was an opening in a distant land, South Africa. Actually, South Africa was not quite alien to Indians. A considerable number had gone there to do farm work and to engage in trade. The country was inhabited largely by black-skinned people belonging to the Bantu groups, who were strictly ruled by a comparatively small number of Dutch and English.

Gandhi heard that many Indians in South Africa were doing well, particularly as traders. However, most of them were farmhands, working as indentured servants and obligating themselves to remain for a number of years. Their transportation costs were paid in addition to their wages. Even though they may have been treated badly by their white masters, they could at least feed themselves and their families, something which they might not have been able to do in India.

The offer to Gandhi came from a businessman, Abdullah Sheth Karim Ihaveri, a Muslim and a partner in the export and import firm of Dada Abdullah & Co. The firm had branches in two parts of South Africa: the province of Natal and the Orange Free State. The services of young Gandhi were needed in connection with a case involving some forty thousand pounds—the equivalent of about two hundred thousand dollars at that time—stemming from a complicated business transaction. Gandhi was to aid the firm's attorneys, to perform odd chores, and also to work as a scribe.

He was offered a salary of one hundred and five pounds a year—about five hundred dollars—a modest sum even then. His tour of duty would probably last only one year. If he had been successful at home, Gandhi might have hesitated, but he had not been. What could he gain in South Africa? He did not know, but perhaps the year's tour of duty would give him another chance to find himself. It would certainly enlarge his horizon. Gandhi accepted the offer. He could not possibly know what part South Africa was to play in his life, and in the future of his native land.

It was on a hot April day in 1893 that Gandhi again left his family and took the boat from India. Bombay was wrapped in its blast-furnace heat. This time the majority of fellow passengers were Gandhi's countrymen, headed for South Africa. They were indentured servants, undertaking seven years of work for tiny wages. Should they leave their service they would be treated as criminals and put in jail. After seven years, they could either stay in South Africa and receive a small parcel of land, or return to their homes at their masters' cost. The Indians looked lean and morose. At best, their future was dark. The only hope was more food than at home and a lenient master.

These indentured servants were headed either for Natal, a British colony, or the adjacent Orange Free State, which was a republic run by Afrikaners, descendants of Dutch settlers.

The white man—English and Dutch—had taken possession of South Africa, even though the majority of the inhabitants were black-skinned natives. The white people used an Arab word to refer to the natives, calling them *Kaffirs*, which means "pagan." Although the natives tried to resist the white man's intrusion, they could not stand up against superior arms.

At that period in his life, Gandhi was not a politically minded man. He had only hazy notions about South Africa's racial problems. He had heard that the whites discriminated against colored people, including the people from India. But he thought little of that. He felt that conditions could not have been very bad, because so many Indians had left their country to work in South Africa, and they would not have done so if the conditions had been intolerable.

The ship sailed southwestward into equatorial waters, crossed the Equator, and entered the southern hemisphere. More days passed and the ship left the tropics, crossing the Tropic of Capricorn, and was back again in the temperate zone. At last they arrived at Durban, with its lovely, warm climate. From there Gandhi had to continue his trip inland to Johannesburg, where he was to meet his employers.

When the ship docked, the masters' stewards called for the indentured servants, barely looking at them. They merely read off their names, then lined them up and marched them off. The stewards were hefty people with white skin and pink cheeks, the type that Gandhi had seen in England. But they were not as friendly as the English, and not one of them gave a welcome nod to the Indians.

This was the first African city that Gandhi had ever seen. The shore was fringed with palms, just as at home in Porbandar, but in Durban the air was not so hot. On the contrary, it was invigorating, and the white people in the streets walked with a swagger. Obviously, this was the white man's country.

Gandhi had never seen as beautiful a town as Durban. It was spotlessly clean; the white walls of the well-built houses gleamed in the rays of the sun. There were parks every few blocks, filled with scented flowers, and the public buildings looked most impressive. The city appeared to be the home of well-to-do men.

In 1893 there was no continuous rail line from Durban to Johannesburg as there is today. Gandhi could travel by rail only part of the way; then he would have to take a stagecoach, and continue to Johannesburg by way of Ladysmith. At that point the coach would cross the boundary of the Orange Free State, travel a small part of the northeast portion, cross the frontier again into Transvaal, and continue through Germiston and Pretoria to Johannesburg.

At the outset all seemed to go well, and young Gandhi had no reason to anticipate trouble. He found an empty compartment in the railway car, and took a window seat to look at the beautiful landscape.

When the train stopped at Pietermaritzburg, the door of the compartment was roughly opened and in came one of the hefty white settlers whose self-confidence had impressed Gandhi in Durban. The settler looked him over critically and apparently disliked what he saw. As suddenly as he had come he left, but not for long. When he returned, he was accompanied by two railway officials. One of them, who seemed to be the man in charge, wore a gold-braided cap, and he addressed Gandhi gruffly.

"You must leave this compartment."

Gandhi protested. "I have a valid ticket for this trip, and there is nobody else in this compartment."

Gandhi suspected that the white man did not like his dark color. But this was an English-speaking country; he had lived in England and had encountered no such treatment there.

"It makes no difference," the official answered, his

pink cheeks becoming red as if Gandhi's meek remark had been an insult. "You must leave this compartment and proceed to the baggage van."

"I don't want to, and I have the right to stay here."

"You don't want to, but I insist."

The two officials grabbed Gandhi and removed him from the car. They were about to take him into the baggage car by way of the station platform, but Gandhi rebelled, kicking and shouting. The officials thereupon took him into the waiting room and dropped him on a bench. Then they left. No sooner did they leave the waiting room than the man in authority gave the signal for the train to depart, leaving Gandhi alone. Now there was no one to listen to his protest. He could leave town only by waiting until the following day for the next train.

Gandhi spent the entire night in the waiting room. The town was located high in the mountains, and Gandhi, used to the furnacelike heat of India, found the air distressingly cold. The following day he continued his trip to the end of the line. There he got his ticket for the stagecoach, but soon ran into trouble again.

He took a seat inside the coach bound for Johannesburg. But the "leader" of the coach ordered him to sit on the outside footboard. Gandhi protested with vehemence, determined not to let himself be cowed again. The "leader" began to shove the frail Indian, and fellow passengers had to shield him from possible harm.

Finally, a very unhappy young traveler reached his destination in Johannesburg. He was not met at the coach station because of the mix-up the night before. Gandhi arrived alone, late in the evening, at the Grand National Hotel, and asked for a room. Looking him over critically, the reception clerk told him that no accommodation was available. Right behind Gandhi stood an Afrikaner—a Boer—who had no trouble getting a room. Eventually Gandhi did get a place in which to spend the night, but not at the Grand National Hotel.

When he related his misadventures to his Indian employers, they said, "We can match your stories with woes of our own. But we became used to them and so will you. People with European backgrounds are very color-conscious here, and the settlers of Dutch ancestry even more so than the British. Most of us have learned to live with them. While we have to pocket their insults, we also have a chance to pocket their money."

Thus was Gandhi introduced to the treatment which the South African whites gave to those whose skin was a darker color. The young Indian had always thought that he belonged to the white race. He was not a Negro nor a Mongoloid. But to most of the South African settlers, Gandhi was a man of color. They looked down upon the Indians, whom they called "Samies" or "coolies," terms usually applied to the Chinese. After Gandhi's experience in England, where he encountered no such discrimination, he greatly disliked the treatment given to him, but he comforted himself with the thought that his stay in South Africa would be short.

Gandhi worked hard for his employers. The lawsuit for which he was called to South Africa proved to be a long one, dragging on endlessly. He spent much time on the case, and the more he thought about it, the more he became convinced that the only solution was a compromise. He drew up a plan which he thought to be fair, and presented it to the principals involved. First they thought little of it, but the plan did make sense and Gandhi kept bringing it to his employer's attention with increasing self-confidence. When they finally realized that it was the best solution, they accepted it.

Gandhi was overjoyed at the result. He saw the lawsuit not merely from the point of view of his employers but in a much broader context.

"My joy was boundless at the outcome of the case," he wrote. "I had learned the meaning of the true practice of law. I realized that the lawyer's true function was to bring together the parties riven asunder."

However, not all barristers agreed with this view. What would happen to their profession if controversies were never to reach the courts? But there were others who were impressed by Gandhi's ideas. Foremost among these were the Gujarati Indians of Johannesburg. They formed a tight little community with a "grapevine" of its own, which rapidly carried news to its members. This grapevine helped them to become acquainted with Gandhi's name. Karamchand Gandhi was already known to some of them, and that also helped to bring the son to their attention. The Gujarati learned that this young man in their midst, with an English law degree, was not interested in dragging out cases as were so many other barristers. Word soon spread that Gandhi cared more for truth than for a high income. Then another incident took place which further enhanced his reputation.

Gandhi agreed to handle a case, believing that his client's representation of the facts was true. After going into the minute details, Gandhi realized that his client had lied. When the case came up for trial, Mohandas Gandhi addressed the court.

"Your Honor, I move that my client's case be dismissed without any further argument," he said.

The judge commended the young attorney for his integrity. The crestfallen client asked Gandhi's forgiveness for having attempted to lead him astray.

Young Gandhi learned a lasting lesson from cases like this one. "It is not important to win a case, but it is important to find the truth." He realized that truth was often subject to various interpretations. But it could be found in most cases by applying common sense. He learned that many conflicts in the lawcourts could be avoided by engaging in give and take. It was possible to gain more sometimes by giving than by taking. Truth was bound to win in the end.

Even though increasing numbers of fellow Gujaratis became familiar with Gandhi's work, he had no plan to remain in South Africa. He completed the task for which he had come and now he was ready to go back to India to be with his family.

Then he noticed the headline of a short news item entitled "Indian Franchise." It mentioned a bill before the Natal legislature aimed at the disfranchisement of Indian residents. They now had the right to vote as did the whites, but they would lose it if the bill became law.

When Gandhi's employers learned about the bill, they realized that if it were passed, they would have no voice in their future. They had planned a farewell party for Gandhi, but at the party they asked him to postpone his return and to form a one-man lobby to fight the bill.

"Shri Gandhi," the spokesman said, "this piece of news disturbs us. In spite of the social discrimination against us, we have not been doing poorly in this country. But if this bill is made law, we will become second-class citizens. Then other such laws may be passed against us. We think that the time has come to make a stand. Also we think that you are the man to be our spokesman. This will be full-time work, necessitating the postponement of your return. Naturally we are ready to guarantee your fee, if you stay."

"The fee is unimportant," Gandhi answered, "but, as you know, my family is at home and I wish to join them."

The employers' spokesman was Abdullah Sheth, the

man who had been instrumental in Gandhi's call to Africa. Although much older than Gandhi, Abdullah Sheth addressed him with the respect that a young person owes to an older man.

"*Gandhibai* (father Gandhi)," he told him, "we are aware of your family duties, and we do not wish to make it impossible for you to perform them. All we ask is that you stay here for one month, in order to get this thing started. As business people, we are not very good in dealing with authorities. Our minds do not work that way. Please stay."

Gandhi accepted the invitation and declared that he needed no fee.

Many of the Indians were men of money. Abdullah Sheth turned to them. "Friends," he said, "Gandhibai wants no fee from us and we have to respect his wish. But he must live, and send funds to his family. Also, he will incur some expenses for printing leaflets, sending telegrams, traveling around the country, and consulting books that we must buy. Furthermore, one man is not enough for this work and so he will have to engage aid. All this takes money, and we must help."

Most of the Indians present were Muslims, and they replied, "Allah is merciful and great; the money will be available. Gandhibai will have as much help as he needs. Please consent to stay, and all will be well."

"Very well then, friends," Gandhi replied. "I will stay for a month, and then you will take over. I'll cancel my return passage to Bombay, and send word to my family to be patient for a while longer."

So the farewell party was turned into a welcoming party. In the end, Gandhi stayed for longer than one month. Thus, his role in history began.

4

The Force of Truth

Gandhi launched a campaign to combat the discriminatory "Indian Franchise" bill. The bill was unjust, and he soon became familiar with all the arguments. He felt eloquence swelling within him as he held imaginary dialogues with the authorities. Could he get to them? Would they listen to him? And if they did, what would be their reactions? He would come to them as a petitioner, hat in hand, and perhaps he again might become flustered.

Many years later, he explained the steps that he had taken in South Africa. He spoke in a language that reminded his admirers of the Testaments.

"Look at a flower," he said. "It has certain traits, shape, color, consistency, and scent. It consists of millions, nay, myriads of cells, combined in a way that provide its unique traits. What would the flower be without the binding force? Heaps of ingredients without shape, color, consistency, and scent. And what accounts for its being a flower, that particular kind of flower—organization. And look at all the other objects in life—animate and inanimate. They are masterpieces of organization. There is an infinity of combinations of comparatively few ingredients.

"We should learn from nature. Man appears to us the greatest masterpiece of organization. We are unique. We are so created that we can imitate the handiwork of God. It is said that we are created in His image among all the living creatures and I believe this is true. Man can organize, as God can. God endowed us with the capacity of organization and indeed imposed the obligation upon us to use it for our betterment. We are social creatures who find fulfillment by using our capacity to organize. Individually we are inchoate cells, as are the ingredients of flowers. Organized, we acquire the power of giants in fulfillment of our destiny."

Organization was the road to success. As an individual, Mohandas K. Gandhi could not combat discrimination, but as the spokesman of an organization, he could. Gandhi organized fund-raising means, and aroused public opinion. Some of the Indians in South Africa were influential men who, as an organized pressure group, represented a force which the authorities could not ignore. The government could not allow the Indian settlers to upset Natal's economy.

Gandhi named his organization the Natal Indian Congress. It was patterned on the Indian National Congress, founded some nine years before to speak for the people of India. This new organization was to speak for Gandhi's people in Natal. He drafted his first petition in its name and submitted it to the Natal parliament. However, there were some impetuous people among Gandhi's countrymen who advocated stronger measures. Suppose the legislature paid no attention to the petitioners? They pointed to examples of successful stands against injustice in the Western world. They called attention to the Swiss in Europe and to the people of the United States, both of whom had been subject to oppression, and had risen against their oppressors and won their rights.

"True enough," Gandhi countered, "but they formed the majority. We are a minority—a minority among the whites and more so among the blacks."

"But the black Bantus and ourselves make a majority."

"True again," Gandhi replied, "but the Bantus have not approached us to fight in their name. They will have to struggle for their own rights."

"That is so, Gandhibai; but what do you suggest? Why the Natal Indian Congress then? We might just as well give up the fight."

"Not at all," Gandhi answered. "We cannot fight the Europeans with force, but we can try to do so with the force of truth. People are often unjust because they do not know where justice lies. We can try to convince the Europeans that they will prosper more if they let us have

73

a hand in bettering the general welfare. This may be of help to the black people, too. Eventually, the Europeans will see that we are right, and living standards will rise all around. Then they may also realize that a country is better off if all of its people live well, not one-tenth rich and nine-tenths poor."

"Allah is merciful," fellow Indians said, "and has rewarded us with Gandhibhai. Truly, he is Allah's gift to us."

Gandhi sincerely believed that force would not work. But if not violence, then what? His thoughts turned to Indian history, and especially to Emperor Asoka, 273–232 B.C., who ruled over much of the Indian subcontinent. At first the Emperor gained his realm by force. Then Asoka had a vision that changed his ways. The vision showed him a land in which there was no bloodshed, no mothers' tears for their sons. In the ninth year of his reign, Asoka became a Buddhist and began a search for *Sadbuddhi*, Great Wisdom. He found it by sheathing his sword and establishing a new guide for conduct: "Truth always wins, while violence loses." The age of his physical conquests was over, and India's Golden Age began. It was perhaps not as golden as legend says, but it was better for the people than it had been during the time of the wars.

A great contemporary also affected Gandhi's thinking at that time. He was Count Leo Tolstoi, the Russian writer. Few books had made a more profound impression on Gandhi than Tolstoi's *War and Peace,* which showed war in a new light. The famous novel said that there were no winners in war, only losers. War destroyed not only the bodies of people but also their minds, contradicting the eternal truth that human life was sacred.

Gandhi read Tolstoi's other writings, too, and then wrote to him, calling him his guru. From distant Russia came the writer's reply. "Only truth keeps man's spiritual forces alive; it is the only effective weapon to win a cause. Violence will never help a cause. It is the law of nature that construction is never affected by destructive means."

So the influences of Emperor Asoka, of Leo Tolstoi, and of his own experiences in South Africa helped Mohandas Gandhi to reach the conclusion which was to gain him world fame, creating a new school of thought in modern times. It was summarized in an Indian word which became known throughout the globe—*satyagraha.* *Satya* means truth; *agraha* means force. The two together —truth force—proclaim that truth is the only effective force. Linked to it was the pledge never to use force, which Gandhi called *ahimsa*—no violence. The Gandhi "lobby" in South Africa was the first use of satyagraha.

The month which Gandhi was to have spent in South Africa was now gone, and yet his work had barely begun. Although he was anxious to rejoin his family, he could not leave his unfinished work. He saw now that one month was far from sufficient to begin "Operation Truth."

Meanwhile, the Natal legislature was determined to go ahead with its plan of disfranchising the Indian settlers. Gandhi realized that not only the problem of depriving his countrymen of their vote was at stake—the greater issue involved universal human rights.

Months passed, and Gandhi found himself in the midst of a campaign that he could not drop. He was surprised to find the Natal Britishers inflexible. At home the Englishmen had listened to arguments. What accounted for the difference? Gandhi wondered. Was it that at home they felt secure? In South Africa, on the other hand, they occupied the black man's country, and since they formed a small minority, they might have been unsure of themselves. Their insecurity aroused an aggressive stand, and they became inflexible.

Since Natal was a British possession, Gandhi decided to present the case of his countrymen not only to the local legislature but also to English public opinion. After all, the final decision in political matters rested in London's hands. He prepared a strong "brief" against the proposed discriminatory legislation regarding the Indians, and called it the "Green Pamphlet" for the color of its cover. He sent it to the members of the Natal legislature and to influential people, including newspaper editors in Britain, hoping that it would arouse not only their attention but also their sympathy. He did not foresee the consequences.

As more months passed, he realized that his work

might take years. Now he wanted to return to India to bring Kasturbai and the boys to South Africa. In 1896 he asked permission of the Indian community in Durban for six months' leave, and his request was granted. He had been away from his native land for three years.

People in India had heard about Gandhi's work and they wanted to see him. When he had returned from London he had been met only by his kin; now he was met by an entire delegation bringing the compliments of the Indian National Congress, whose interest had been aroused by his work. The Indians were particularly intrigued by ahimsa and satyagraha. How successful had Gandhi's work been, and how did the people react to his Green Pamphlet?

After visiting his home, Gandhi was whisked off on a tour of India to tell the people about his work. He told them of the abuse to which Indians were subjected in South Africa. The condition of the Indians in the Transvaal, then part of a Boer republic, was even worse than in Natal. There people of color—and Indians were considered as such—had to carry "passes" from their masters if they wished to leave their dwellings after nightfall. What if one had no master, as in the case of a lawyer, physician, or businessman? Then the person had to ask any white man to sign such a pass. People of color were treated like children; whites were considered mature.

Gandhi also told his audiences what the Natal Indian Congress was doing to arouse the conscience of fair-minded whites and to create favorable public opinion against abuse. It was a long-term project, the completion of which would take years.

Many people in Gandhi's audiences felt that a man like Gandhi was needed in India, too, where the British held a tight string. While India had no "pass laws," it also had no franchise for Indians. A few thousand Britishers decided what hundreds of millions of Indians were to do. Would ahimsa work on the peninsula? Would satyagraha work?

But Gandhi had no time to linger. His obligation was to return to South Africa. The six months' leave was about to expire. Again he was at the gateway of India, accompanied this time by Kasturbai and their two children. Harilal was now eight, and Manilal, four. They took the HMS *Courland*, a ship in the regular Bombay–Durban service of the Peninsular and Oriental line. However, the voyage was not "regular" at all.

While Gandhi was visiting India, his Green Pamphlet had reached Britain. A copy had landed on the editorial desk of Reuters, the British Empire's worldwide news syndicate. The syndicate editors distilled the contents of the pamphlet into a few paragraphs, emphasizing its strongest points. The news item was then distributed among the subscribers throughout the entire British Empire. The dispatch reached Durban and was published there. It gave the impression that Gandhi had indicted all of Natal and all of South Africa for cruelty and in-

justice. The publication created a great stir, arousing
many people.

Besides the *Courland* there was another ship from
Bombay bound for Durban with a large Indian passenger
list. Normally, the boats were cleared promptly, their
passengers allowed to go their way. But not this time.
The Natal authorities wanted to take their revenge on
Gandhi and on all Indians. Therefore they kept both
ships outside of the harbor, supposedly in quarantine
because of an outbreak of plague in Bombay. False ru-
mors spread in town, and the population of Durban was
incensed. People thought that Gandhi had come back
with an Indian force to invade the country.

For twenty-three days the two ships were kept outside
of the port. Meanwhile, agitators in Durban were at work
to give Gandhi a reception such as he had never seen.

After the long wait, the other passengers, including
Gandhi's family, were allowed to leave, but not Gandhi.
Finally the boat had to sail back and so Gandhi was allowed to leave, too. There was a "reception committee"
on hand when he landed. The place of Gandhi's destination in Durban was the home of a client and friend, Rus-
tomji Sheth, and Gandhi hailed a ricksha pulled by a
Zulu to take him there.

When the Zulu saw an angry crowd begin to surround
Gandhi, he gasped *"Kha"* (no), and broke away.

Gandhi now had to go on foot, surrounded by the hostile mob, which began to throw stones and knock him to

the ground. By the time he reached West Street, the main thoroughfare, the crowd was large. A huge man came up to Gandhi, slapped his face, and kicked him. Had Gandhi not held on to the railing of a house, he would have fallen. But he recovered his balance and continued on.

Recollecting the event, Gandhi was to note later, "I had almost given up the hope of reaching home alive. But I remember well that even then my heart did not arraign my assailants."

The crowd grew still larger. When the danger appeared to be the greatest, help reached him. The wife of the superintendent of police, who knew and respected Gandhi, happened to pass by. She took him under her protection as the crowd stood aside. With this escort, Gandhi reached the house of his friend. But the danger was not over.

Now the troublemakers converged on the friend's house. Meanwhile, the police superintendent's wife had managed to inform her husband of the danger, and he came with a group of men. He mounted the porch of the house to address the people, telling them that Durban could not put up with such lawlessness. The angry surging mob paid no attention to him. Then the superintendent, while keeping the attention of the crowd, had Gandhi dressed as a member of the local police. Thus disguised, the Indian was taken out of the house to safety.

Soon after, Gandhi was interviewed. He told reporters

that the newspaper version of the Green Pamphlet, which had aroused the crowd's anger, had been badly garbled. The newspapers reported the interview and confirmed the truth of Gandhi's statement. This quieted the town, which now decided to ignore Gandhi.

News of these events reached London, too. The colonial secretary there was Joseph Chamberlain, who found such lawlessness intolerable in a British possession. He issued instructions to the Durban authorities to indict the ringleaders, if necessary. These developments enhanced Gandhi's reputation in South Africa, India, and even in England.

The public prosecutor in Natal asked Gandhi to provide him with the details of the incident.

"The only detail I can give you is this," Gandhi replied. "The attackers did beat me up, as you can see, and they may have had murder in their minds. But they were ignorant hoodlums acting upon their impulses, with no thoughts in their minds. I cannot blame them any more than I would blame naughty children."

"Mr. Gandhi," the public prosecutor said, "you are probably right. Crowds like this do not contain responsible people. Let us hope that your generosity will be a lesson, and that those hoodlums will see how far superior you are to them."

This incident again increased Gandhi's stature not only in the local Indian community but also in the government of Natal. London now looked upon Gandhi as the representative of the Indian community in South Africa.

It was under the challenge of these events that Gandhi, formerly so timid, earned the reputation of being an especially courageous man. He found numerous admirers even among the white population.

In the year of Gandhi's return, South Africa witnessed an event called the Jameson Raid, which greatly affected the young Indian's life.

Enterprising Dutch people had settled in the southernmost tip of Africa as far back as the mid-seventeenth century. They had hoped to make a living by growing food for the ships' crews of the Dutch East Indies Company, sailing between the Netherlands and the Indies. The Dutch word for farmer is *boer*, and so the settlers came to be known as Boers. (The same word had been used to denote Dutch farmers in North America, too.)

When the British became the strongest power in India, they took over the South African supply route. The Boers then decided to seek their fortunes in the vast open regions of the north beyond the river Vaal, called Transvaal, and the adjacent Orange River country. The Boers would probably have lived happily if it had not become known that some of their territory contained the world's largest diamond and gold mines. At that time, the great British pioneer Cecil Rhodes was establishing an English colony to the north, later to become Rhodesia. Because of the mines, British forces, led by Leander Starr Jameson, and aided by Rhodes, invaded the Transvaal. This led to war between the British and the Boers—the Boer War, or South African War, of 1899.

Gandhi and his countrymen found themselves in the midst of the conflict. Natal, the main Indian settlement, was British, while the Orange Free State, adjacent to Natal and headed by a Boer government, joined the Transvaal. Although Gandhi believed in ahimsa, no violence, he also believed that as a British subject he had certain obligations. Therefore, he organized an ambulance corps of eleven hundred members to minister to the needs of the British casualties. This corps went so deep into the thick of battle that many of its members were lost. Moving with great rapidity, the corps sometimes covered twenty-five miles a day. Its work attracted favorable attention not only among the British in South Africa, but also in England. "They are sons of the Empire after all," the *Times* of London commented. Gandhi's fame grew another notch due to his ambulance corps.

The bitter war aroused worldwide attention. The great British Empire found it difficult to subdue a small country of embattled peasants, for the Boers exhibited remarkable fighting qualities. After much effort, the British won, and peace was restored on May 31, 1902.

In spite of their victory, the British realized that the Boers would not remain peacefully under colonial rule. As a result, England allowed South Africa a large measure of self-government. The Afrikaners—those who spoke the

Boer language—and English-speaking British settlers patched up their quarrels and lived together in peace. Natal, Transvaal, and the Cape of Good Hope became provinces of the Dominion of South Africa.

Before the war started, the Gandhis had a third son. Their fourth and last child, a boy, was born when the war was a year old. The names of the children indicated the father's religious feelings. Gandhi called his third son Ramdas (the Servant of Rama), whom Gandhi considered the Supreme Being. Always in moments of great crisis, he invoked Rama's aid. The name he gave to his fourth son was Devadas (the Servant of God).

Gandhi, now in his early thirties and with a respected name, was not yet sure of his future career. He was drawn to South Africa, but now there was stirring on the Indian political scene. Gandhi decided to return to India, still leaving the door open to South Africa.

He told his South African friends that if they needed him, he would be at their call. Then he took Kasturbai and the four boys—the youngest was now a year old—and returned to India.

Gandhi wanted to aid his countrymen at home, and so he established contact with the Indian National Congress, attending its annual meeting in Calcutta. He was not happy with what he saw. The Congress did not strike him as the spokesman for India's vast masses. Most of the people at Calcutta were well-fed professionals, mainly lawyers who knew little about the villagers' lives. When, for instance, Gandhi asked a delegate from the state of Bikaner about its famine, the man knew nothing about it. When Gandhi talked to a delegate of the Bilaspur District in the Central Provinces, the officeholder did not seem to know about the deep discontent of the peasants against the estate owners who exploited them. Gandhi wanted to see peasants among the Congress party members.

From Calcutta, he proceeded to Bombay, where he hoped to feel "India's heartbeat," and where he felt most at home. Since he considered remaining in India, he had to make his living there. He opened a law office. But there was no throng of clients in his waiting room, in spite of the modest fame he had gained. He also encountered professional jealousy. His fellow barristers considered him an intruder.

However, soon the call came again from South Africa, where conditions had deteriorated further.

This time Gandhi's destination was Johannesburg, popularly known as "Jo," which had become an important center for Asian settlers. There was now a direct rail line between Natal and Jo. The city was a great industrial hub, surrounded by factories and miners' compounds. Gandhi took a house in the suburb of Doornfontein, and opened his law office at the corner of Rissek and Anderson streets. His inside office was sparsely furnished and he had a lady typist in the modest waiting room.

By now Gandhi's name was magic to his fellow Indians in South Africa, and so clients came in great numbers. Some of his clients were extremely rich. They turned to Gandhi as their spokesman to fight discrimination in high places.

While working in his office, Gandhi found time to prepare for a still broader career. This time, too, it was a book that changed his future. It had been given to him by an English friend, Henry S. L. Polak, about whom Gandhi was to write: "We seemed to hold closely similar views on the essential things of life." The title of the book was *Unto This Last*, written by John Ruskin, the British art critic. Gandhi said that the book opened his eyes to the spiritual mysteries of life.

From it he learned that nobody could flourish in isolation from his fellow human beings and still be contented. Nor could one thrive at the expense of his fellowman. The better off the fellowman was, the better off he would be, because human fates were linked. We are all our brothers' keepers.

Gandhi learned another lesson from Ruskin's book. "Manual labor was noble, even more so than 'white-collar' work." This was a great revelation to Gandhi, the product of a caste-conscious land. "The barber's work has no less value than that of a lawyer," Ruskin had said. A barber doing his work well deserved more respect than a barrister performing his task poorly. Respect should be paid to the person, to the laborer, not to the labor.

Ruskin gave Gandhi still a third lesson. The life of the tiller of the soil was particularly noble, according to him. Food is life and the food producer is the dispenser of life. Being close to nature on the land, the farmer is closest to its changeless truths, the embodiment of which is God.

"This book," Gandhi commented, "brought about an instantaneous and practical transformation of my life." To him it was not just *a* book. It was *the* book, and he reacted to it with enthusiasm.

He could not sleep for nights, feeling that he had to apply the lessons he had learned. But how was he to do it? He was not content with learning merely for learning's sake. He tried to organize his thoughts, preliminary to organizing his deeds.

"Modern life tends to be unnatural," he reflected. "People live in large cities, cut off from air, engaged in occupations behind closed doors. Being isolated from nature, they lead unnatural lives, stepping on one another's feet in crowded urban centers. They should turn to nature, live on the land, where there is more space. They should produce basic products, also engage in handicrafts enabling them to employ their imagination and skills."

With these thoughts, Gandhi organized Phoenix Farm in 1904 on the outskirts of Durban. He founded it to help his people move closer to nature—himself and his family included. Phoenix was the name of the mythical bird which rose from the ashes after having been consumed by flames. A new way of life was to rise from the ashes of an unnatural civilization.

Phoenix Farm consisted at first of some twenty acres of land with orange and mango trees clustering around a spring. Another eighty acres of adjacent land had more fruit trees and a cottage. Gandhi bought that, too. A thousand pounds was the price for all this area. He began a sugarcane farm and invited nearby Indian residents to try their fortunes. He would alternate between his office and the farm. It was Gandhi's idea that a teacher, for instance, might want to double as a gardener, or a gardener as a teacher. This type of life might provide new stimulation to the settlers, while enhancing their overall usefulness.

From then on, places like Phoenix Farm played significant parts in Gandhi's life. He used a Sanskrit word to identify them: *ashram*, a place of retreat. In the ashram, the people were to engage in work, meditating, exchanging ideas with fellow workers and learning to lead the life that Ruskin envisaged in *Unto This Last*.

Gandhi installed a flatbed press on the farm. He used it for the weekly issues of his newspaper *Indian Opinion*, the first and only publication of the Indian settlers in South Africa. It contained news of interest to them in Africa, interspersed with sketches of events in India. Copies of the weekly were also mailed to the South African authorities, in an attempt to acquaint them with the problems of the Indian community.

Soon Gandhi had to face a special problem. The government of Transvaal, now a self-governing province, published a proposed ordinance in its official *Gazette* in August, 1906. It would require all Indians to be fingerprinted and to carry special certificates of identification at all times. In those days, only criminals were fingerprinted. Imprisonment and deportation were threatened to those who failed to comply. Gandhi felt that this ordinance, named "The Black Act," would mean ruin for the Indians of South Africa if enacted, because it would be merely the first step in a campaign of constant harassment and discrimination.

To fight The Black Act, a meeting was called in the Empire Theatre of Johannesburg, on September 11, 1906, a day destined to be a landmark in the history of the Indian community. Delegates from all over the Transvaal attended the meeting, and the theater was packed. Gandhi noticed the expectation on every face. The chairman of the Transvaal British Indian Association, Abdul Gani, an Indian Muslim, presided. He was one of the community's oldest residents and a partner in the well-known firm of Mamad Kasam Kamrudin, an export-import house.

As the most highly respected member of the Indian community, Mohandas Gandhi was the main speaker, and he submitted several proposals to the gathering, most important of which was named the "Fourth Resolution." It proclaimed the determination of the Indian residents not to submit to the proposed ordinance even if it became the law of the land. Because of the diverse backgrounds of the audience members, the meeting was conducted in Hindi, Gujarati, Tamil, and Telegu, four of India's hundreds of languages and dialects.

One speaker was the experienced "old South Africa" hand, Sheth Haji Habib, who made an impassioned plea to the audience to take an oath to resist degrading legislation. This was a matter of high principle, he said, far beyond the line which any government had the right to draw. The government's proposal was an infringement of human rights.

More than any other participant, Gandhi realized the significance of the resolution. While he was in favor of taking the oath, he also wanted the people at the mass meeting to realize what risks they were about to take. "We may have to go to jail," he told them, "where we may be affronted. There we may have to go hungry and suffer extreme heat or cold. Also, hard labor may be imposed upon us, and we may be flogged. Those among us who are opulent today may be reduced to abject poverty. We might be deported. Suffering from starvation and similar hardships in jail, some of us may fall ill and even die. We may have to endure every imaginable hardship. If we take this pledge, we must understand the consequences. In the face of all the cruelty we face, we must hold our own."

An unjust law was not a law in God's eyes, the assemblage replied. Its victims were under no obligation to observe it. On the contrary, it was the citizen's duty to resist unjust laws. But it was to be resistance without violence—passive resistance.

Gandhi wanted to have an Indian name for this important phase of his people's struggle for humane treatment, and he announced in the *Indian Opinion* that a prize would be given to the reader who suggested the best name for it. One of the competitors was Gandhi's second cousin, Maganlal Gandhi, who suggested the word *Sadagraha*, meaning "firmness in a good cause." Gandhi liked the general idea but not the particular designation, and he changed it to *Satyagraha*, the force of truth. Implied in the motto was Gandhi's conviction that even in a just cause, violence never wins. Satyagraha now became the hallmark of Gandhiism, the essence of his practical philosophy, a political concept with religious undertones.

Despite the opposition of the Indian community, The Black Act became law. Steadfast to his oath, Gandhi refused to be fingerprinted and registered. He and many of his countrymen were arrested and tried. Gandhi was sentenced to two months in jail. He entered the prison on a January day in 1908. This was his first jail term, but for more than a generation he was to be an inmate of many jails. Although he was neither starved nor tortured in prison, it was a hard test just the same. When free, walking was his only exercise, but now he was shut up in a cell which he described as "a safe-deposit box," its door made of solid iron. The cell had no window and air reached him only through a small opening beneath the ceiling. The cell door was locked for the night at six in the afternoon.

In jail, Gandhi continued to be his countrymen's spokesman. He petitioned the authorities to grant the prisoners the privilege of exercising in the prison yard. The request was granted after some delay, and so the monotony of detention was broken. Also, the yard exercises added a dash of humor to the prisoners' drab lives.

Their drillmaster was a fellow prisoner, Nawabkhan, a Pathan tribesman from India's mountainous northwest region. The mountaineer had unlimited lung power, but only a limited knowledge of English, which the prisoners, speaking different tongues, had adopted as their common language. When the Pathan wanted the prisoners to relax, he shouted "Soundlies." The men guessed what he wanted—that they may stand at ease—but they were puzzled about the meaning of the strange sound. Eventually they learned that "Soundlies" stood for "Stand at Ease."

During one exercise period, a prison guard handed Gandhi an official paper. It was sent to him by a member of the government, General Jan Christiaan Smuts. It contained Gandhi's release from prison and an invitation to a conference concerning complaints of the Indian settlers. The authorities had recognized Gandhi as the Transvaal Indian residents' spokesman even in jail.

From then on General Smuts had many dealings with Gandhi. Smuts had fought on the Boer side against the British, but had made his peace with England and had become the most respected South African statesman of the British Commonwealth. He was an impressive figure, tall and erect. Now a member of the Transvaal government, he received the ex-convict in his government chambers as an equal. Smuts knew of Gandhi's reputation among the Indians. He summoned him on behalf of his government to offer "a deal." The Indians in Transvaal should comply with the provisions of the law, and thus save embarrassment to the government. After they had registered, the government would repeal The Black Act.

Gandhi had seldom faced such a dilemma. He had taken a pledge, together with many others, to engage in passive resistance against the law; now he was asked to accept the same law. Of course, the acceptance was only to be for a short time.

Gandhi considered an oath as a sacred pledge. But here was a way to make peace with the government, and Gandhi was a man of peace. He did not want his countrymen to have constant quarrels on their hands. After all, they made their living in South Africa, and they could not afford to fight its government forever. The aim of the oath that the Indians had taken was to combat The Black Act, and now General Smuts had promised to have it repealed. Gandhi accepted the offer.

On a radiant summer morning, February 1, 1908,

Gandhi was on his way, accompanied by several country-men, to the government registry office to enter his name in accordance with the Smuts agreement. He was trailed by a Pathan, Mir Alam, who had been one of Gandhi's clients but was now opposed to his policies. Suddenly, the Pathan whipped out a stout stick and struck a heavy blow on Gandhi's head. The Indian collapsed and gasped, exclaiming, *"He, Ram!"* (Oh, God.)

Gandhi was carried into the registry office where a physician revived him. When Gandhi learned his attacker's name, he asked, "Where is he?"

"Under arrest."

"He should be released forthwith. I refuse to press charges against him."

That was not, however, the reaction of the crown's prosecutor, who did press charges against Mir Alam. The attacker was convicted and sentenced to three months in jail.

Gandhi had performed his part of the bargain by registering, and it was now the government's turn. But the government did nothing. Gandhi knew that General Smuts was an honorable man, and so he gave him until August 16 to have the act repealed. However, it remained on the statute books. Had the general gone back on his pledge? He had not, but the provincial legislature had refused to honor his pledge. The legislature had been influenced by a die-hard group of Boers who were to give Smuts many headaches in years to come.

Gandhi decided to call a second satyagraha campaign, which was to begin with a spectacular act—burning the certificates of registration. This time Gandhi wanted the entire world to know about this act of defiance, and he gave it maximum publicity. He organized the burning of the certificates in the largest place at his countrymen's disposal—the courtyard of the Hamidia Mosque in Johannesburg. Every inch of available space was taken up by Indians of all classes. A large caldron resting on four legs—the type in which South African Negroes cooked their meals—was requisitioned from a trader's shop and set up on a high platform. As soon as the caldron was in position, members of the assemblage began to toss thousands of certificates into it. The caldron had been lined with paraffin, and a participant set fire to it. The certificates burst into flames and were reduced to cinders while the spectators cheered.

English newspaper reporters at the meeting were deeply impressed by this spectacular act and they gave graphic descriptions of it in their papers. The Johannesburg correspondent for the *Daily Mail* of London compared the certificate burning with the Boston Tea Party of early American history.

At the ceremony, Gandhi delivered an address which indicated the significance of his life's work.

"No matter what may be said, I will always repeat that this is a struggle for religious freedom. By religion I do not mean formal or customary rituals, but that creed which underlies all religions confronting us with our Maker. If we are to be true to God, we must act like Him, true to our beliefs. If you relinquish your beliefs, you forsake God. To repeat the words of the Jew of Nazareth, those who would follow God have to leave the world, and I call upon my countrymen to leave the world of everyday interests and cling to God, as a child clings to its mother's breast."

The authorities took prompt notice of this act of defiance. For Gandhi's participation in the certificate burning, he was sentenced to two months' imprisonment, which he served at Volksrust, near the Transvaal border. He was rearrested in February, 1909, for his repeated refusal to register, and was sentenced again, this time for three months, which he served partly in Volksrust and partly in Pretoria, later to become the administrative capital of the Union of South Africa.

A few months after his release, Gandhi decided to present his peoples' complaints to the highest authorities in London. He sailed to England and received respectful attention in the English capital, but achieved nothing. The authorities told him that since the Transvaal had self-government in domestic matters, he should present his case to the authorities there.

On his return voyage to South Africa, Gandhi had time to answer those of his countrymen who held that violence was the only language people understood. He condensed his views in a small pamphlet, *Hind Swaraj* (Indian Home

Rule), in his own Gujarati language. It was translated into English and received worldwide attention. Gandhi wrote that the zeal of the extremists was misguided and that violence would never free the Indians either in their homeland or in South Africa. In Gandhi's own words, *Hind Swaraj* attempted to "teach the gospel of love in place of hatred. It wants to replace violence by self-sacrifice. It sets soul force against brute force."

A year after Gandhi's return, the South African provinces merged into the Union of South Africa, a dominion within the British Empire, having the same status as Canada—fully self-governing in domestic matters. Gandhi, who had much respect for the British despite their conduct in India, believed that this merger would help the Indian settlers.

Meanwhile he attended to his work as an attorney, accepting money only for the essential needs of his family. "He will take nothing," his countrymen complained. "The money we had given him in Natal, he handed over to public funds. He is poor because he wants to be poor."

In the midst of work, Gandhi found some leisure time to read and even to establish another ashram. He founded his new retreat in 1910 near Johannesburg, after reading Tolstoi's *The Kingdom of God Is Within You*. Gandhi wrote to Tolstoi a second time in April, 1910, enclosing the latest issue of *Hind Swaraj*. His third and last letter was written August 15, 1910. Tolstoi answered it on the day that he received it, although he was ill. In a long letter, he said that "the longer I live and especially now that I feel so near death, I want to tell others what I feel particularly clearly—the teaching of love uncorrupted by false interpretation—and the justice of passive resistance to unjust governmental acts." Gandhi received this letter on November 21, 1910, a few days after the death of the great novelist. In Tolstoi's memory, Gandhi called his new ashram Tolstoi Farm.

Again the government of the Union of South Africa launched a policy of harassment against those whom it did not consider white. The leaders seemed to feel that only by racial discrimination could the whites keep from being swept away in a tidal wave of nonwhites. This time the government began its attack against the Indians on three different fronts. It banned further Asian immigration; it imposed an annual tax of three pounds on each indentured servant desiring to remain in South Africa after the expiration of his compulsory term of service; finally, it ordered that only marriages performed according to Christian rites would be held legal. The Indians naturally felt that these measures threatened to wipe out their existence in the Union of South Africa. The ban on Asian immigration meant the end of attempts to establish a settled community. As for the tax, most of the indentured laborers were too poor to pay what was then a large amount. The majority of Indians in Africa were married according to Hindu or Muslim rites. If only Christian marriages were legal, then Indian children would be called illegitimate and deprived of their rights. It was the marriage issue which Indian women protested with particular vehemence. Gandhi organized a protest march into Transvaal. He also urged miners to protest against the tax. His plan was to form a march of thousands, whom the authorities would have to arrest. But the marchers could not be held, because of the shortage of jails and the mine owners' need for working hands. The authorities would have to release the arrested people, thereby exposing their unjust laws to public ridicule. The great protest march was to take place in November, 1913.

In that part of South Africa, November weather is much the same as May in the northern hemisphere, a beautiful month and an inducement for people to congregate. Indian indentured servants and the women of India residing in that part of South Africa came from all parts of the Union, from Transvaal and Natal, also from the Orange Free State and the Cape. At the outset, the marching group consisted of two thousand men, over one hundred women, including Gandhi's wife Kasturbai, and about fifty children.

In organizing the march from Natal to Transvaal, Gandhi prepared camps for overnight stops, set up soup kitchens and tents. The marchers tramped along dusty trails, crossing plains, climbing hills, and traversing woods, while singing ancient hymns. The march of the Hindu and Muslim Indians had the air of a pilgrimage.

In Transvaal discrimination against the Indians was

strongest and that is why the marchers would sound their protest there. Before crossing the boundary Gandhi wrote a letter to the authorities, informing them about the object of the pilgrimage. He hoped that to avoid trouble, the government would express its willingness to reconsider its stand. While Gandhi waited for an answer, more thousands joined the satyagraha "army." However, no answer came, and Gandhi gave the signal to begin the great march. At the same time, twenty thousand Indian miners started a strike in Natal.

The marchers crossed the boundary between Natal and Transvaal. Near the frontier, the police were waiting for them at Volksrust. They arrested Gandhi and the other "ringleaders," and took them into a court of justice where a judge imposed a bail of fifty pounds on each arrested leader. That was a large sum in those days, and the judge must have thought that the dust-covered, bedraggled Indians could not pay it. But some of the Indians were wealthy, had cash in hand, and were able to pay the bail for all of them.

Gandhi again joined the marchers, leading them toward Johannesburg. Again he was arrested, this time in the village of Palmford, and again he was released on bond. Wasting no time, he took his place at the head of the marchers once more. The protesters now crossed the river Vaal, and on the other side of the stream, Gandhi was arrested in Standerton. This time the local magistrate came to place the leader under arrest, and a smiling Gandhi bade him welcome.

"I have been promoted," he grinned. "Yesterday I was arrested by a policeman, today by the magistrate himself." The march continued to Teakworth and there Gandhi was arrested again. He thought it was a record.

The procession was to continue to Grailingstad, but at Teakworth Gandhi was put on a train and returned to Natal, then taken to Dundee where he was to be tried on the charge of illegally inducing indentured labor to leave Natal. Other marchers, too, were deported to Natal. At Balfour, several trains had been kept in readiness for the marchers, who were herded into overcrowded cars and taken to Natal. This was not yet the end of the "Great March."

Gandhi was tried in Dundee on November 11, 1913, and sentenced to nine months in jail. Then he was put on another train, taken back to Volksrust in Transvaal, and tried on still another charge. The charge against him was that he had aided and abetted prohibited persons to cross the frontier into Transvaal. This trial took place on the thirteenth, and Gandhi was sentenced to a term of three months. He started to serve his sentence in Volksrust.

Gandhi took these terms of imprisonment in his stride. For the last twenty years of his life, he had had little time to rest. In jail he thought that he would catch up on his readings and, if his warders let him, he would relax. "The prospect of uninterrupted study for a year filled me with joy," he said. His fame was so great by then that he was treated well in jail. He had time to think not only about the present but also about his past and future.

In the midst of his meditations, he was transferred to Bloemfontein in the Orange Free State. There the warden called on him and informed him with a show of respect that he was free. The government wanted to negotiate with Gandhi about the Indians' grievances.

Again General Smuts was his negotiating partner. Smuts felt badly about his earlier failure to live up to his agreement regarding the registration certificates. Throughout the negotiations he manifested great esteem for Gandhi. Finally an agreement was reached between the two men on June 30, 1914, and went into effect the following month. It became known as the "Indian Relief Act." It abolished the annual tax on indentured servants; declared non-Christian marriages valid; and allowed Indians born in South Africa to enter the Cape colony, which was prohibited to them until that time. The act also banned indenture after 1920. This was a triumph for Gandhi and for his nonviolent noncooperation. Satyagraha was vindicated.

At the time, Gandhi was unaware that satyagraha was not the only cause of the agreement. The European diplomatic horizon was another. In 1914, Europe was en-

gaged in a furious arms race, and soon World War I
would erupt. The British government wanted to appease
its Indian subjects in order to keep them quiet at a critical
time.

In the Volksrust jail Gandhi had had time to wonder
about his future. He had become an important person in
South Africa. If the South African government should
agree to the satyagraha demands, what else was he to do?
His own work could be continued by Manilal, his second
son, who had grown up in Africa. Manilal was now over
twenty-one and greatly interested in Phoenix Farm and
in the publication of *Indian Opinion*. Mohandas Gandhi
felt that his own mission in South Africa had been accomplished, and now he was eager to return to his native
land.

After an African stay of over twenty years, Gandhi
booked passage to India, never to return to the "dark
continent." He went home by way of London, to take
another look at the nation of his country's masters. He
knew England to be a sensible country and he hoped to
renew contacts with public officials, then return home,
trying to help both Britain and India by promoting their
friendship. Before the Gandhis left there was a farewell
party which marked the end of an epoch in their lives.
On the eve of their sailing, in July, 1914, Gandhi asked
his Indian friends to give them their blessing, while he
prayed that those who stayed behind would do their duty

to their people, bearing in mind that no reward for a work well done was greater than the approval of their own conscience.

Then Mohandas Gandhi, accompanied by his family, turned his face to the future. He did not realize at the time that he was sailing toward a new destiny and immortality.

Mohandas Karamchand Gandhi (Information Service of India, New York)

Gandhi and his wife Kasturbai in 1921 (International News Photo)

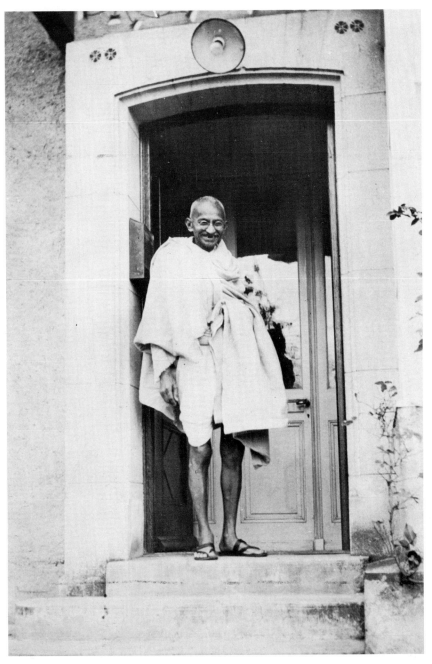

The Mahatma on a visit to Switzerland in 1931 (International News Photo)

Gandhi travels on foot to a peace meeting with Viceroy Lord Irwin in 1931. (International News Photo)

1946 — Gandhi leaves meeting with his arms around his grand-daughter Tara and her friend. At the left is granddaughter Sita, and at the right, Jawaharlal Nehru. (UPI Photo)

Prime Minister Nehru holds a press conference in 1956. He is speaking at India House, London, under a painting of Gandhi. (Information Service of India, New York)

Nehru at his desk in 1963. Note photograph of the Mahatma. (Information Service of India, New York)

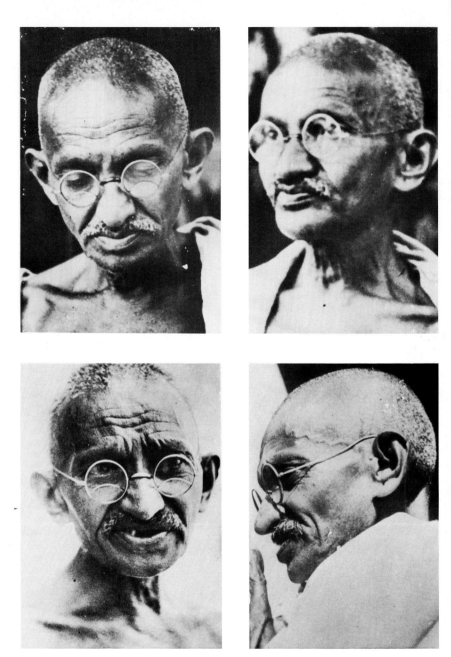

Gandhi at seventy-eight (UPI Photo)

5

Home to India

Gandhi sailed to London by way of Cape Town. A few days before his departure, a young man in a Balkan city murdered Archduke Francis Ferdinand, heir to the thrones of Austria-Hungary. The Indian lawyer had never heard of Francis Ferdinand nor of the city of Sarajevo where the murder had occurred. The event had been reported in the South African press but Gandhi had overlooked it. Sparked by this murder, war broke out suddenly a few days after Gandhi's arrival in England, separating him from his home. History was to call it "the World War."

Soon after Gandhi reached English soil, he organized an Indian Ambulance Corps in London. The scene of the war shifted to northern France, where the British rushed their expeditionary forces to help their French allies against Germany, the ally of Austria-Hungary. Although the English rule in India was distasteful to Gandhi, he realized that he was a British subject and even if his country should become self-governing, he envisaged an India in close contact with Britain. He could not go far with the organization of the ambulance corps, however, because he became ill with pleurisy and had to abandon his project.

Gandhi's first thought after his recovery was to get home to India. Since the start of the war, the seas had not been safe. However, Britain rose rapidly to the challenge and cleared the waters of enemy ships, thereby restoring its globe-encircling lifeline. The passage to India was free again.

Gandhi sailed on HMS *Apollo Bunder*. Fearing possible attack by enemy raiders, the ship's lights were dimmed. It was a ghost ship that sailed the route of the Mediterranean, the Suez Canal, the Red Sea, and finally the Arabian Sea. In the second week of February, 1915, Gandhi caught sight of the familiar landmark, Bombay's majestic marble gateway to India.

When Gandhi reached home, he was still weak from his illness. Even though the sun was warm during the day, he wore a cloak, under which he was dressed in his native garments, a shirt and a loincloth (the *dhoti*) tucked in at the waist. His features looked sharper now, his eyes more protruding, his metal-rimmed glasses straddling the tip of his nose. More than before, he looked like a wise owl, much older than his forty-six years.

Gandhi had expected a few of his kinsmen to meet him at the pier. Looking over the tops of his glasses, he scanned the skyline of Bombay; its magnificent rows of seashore buildings; the Parsi tower of silence; the minarets of the mosque of Bhindi Bazaar; and the Bombay Yacht Club of the English rulers. An important colonial official must be on this boat, Gandhi thought, noticing a huge crowd on the pier. But there was no important colonial official—only Mohandas Karamchand Gandhi, whom the crowd had come to welcome. His fame had preceded him, the fame of a man who had wrested freedom rights for his countrymen from reluctant South African hands. Many people in India already saw him as a man of destiny.

Gandhi's thoughts about the future of his native land, expressed in the *Indian Home Rule,* had attracted much attention in India. Many members of an alert young generation came to see him as their guru. Their "Bible" was Gandhi's book about India in which he had addressed his country's British masters.

"You are my rulers, I concede, and I have no objection to your remaining in my country. But although my rulers now, you will have to become my peoples' servants. It will not be we who have to do what you want us to do but you who have to do what we want. You may keep the riches you have drained from our land but henceforth you may not remove our wealth from us. You may keep order in India, if you wish, but you must relinquish the idea of squeezing our country dry. We consider our civilization superior to yours . . . nor will you be allowed to act contrary to our religions. On account of the Hindus you will have to eschew the enjoyment of beef; because of the Muslims you will have to refrain from eating ham. We want our own courts and schools restored to us, because yours are of no use in our land. Hindi, not English, is India's common language and you will have to learn it.

"We cannot put up with the idea of your spending our money on your railways and military forces. . . . You may fear Russia on account of which you have installed them, but we do not. . . . We will get along with articles produced at home and we have no need for your European clothes. Only if our interests are identical can we work together.

"You, English in India, are not good specimens of your own nation, nor are we, half-Anglicized Indians, good specimens of our nation. You will find that our demands are just if you look up your own scriptures and abandon your own so-called civilization. You may remain in India only if our demands are fulfilled. If you do remain, we will be able to learn from you and you from us."

Gandhi called for self-rule (or home-rule). The road to it was "soul force," however, and not violence. To strengthen India, the country had to have a stronger economy. This could be accomplished through *Swadeshi* (*swa*-self and *deshi*-country)—producing goods in the country itself, thus reducing unemployment, and keeping away the foreign goods that few Indians could afford.

These were bold words, indeed. Home-rule meant self-determination in domestic matters, with the British retaining control of foreign affairs. Also, England would continue to assure peace within the country. But the British would stay in India—according to Gandhi—as servants, not masters.

The people who had come to see Gandhi wanted him to devote his life to doing in India what he had done in South Africa. He was to fight for Indian freedom. Who was to finance his fight? There were plenty of backers, and his personal needs were few. To start his work, Gandhi had to have a foothold from which he could spread the creed of satyagraha.

That foothold was to be a new ashram, a workshop and retreat for meditation, and he set about establishing one on the pattern of the Phoenix Farm in Africa, which now continued to operate under Manilal.

The new retreat would be in the portion of India where Gandhi felt most at home, the Gujarati-speaking country. He established the ashram at Kochrab in the vicinity of Ahmadabad. It was founded with the aid of the Servants of India Society, whose moving spirit was Gopal Krishna Gokhale. Gandhi called this man the "noblest of all Indians." He was a former president of the Congress party and a man of considerable means.

When Indians want to express great respect for a person, they add the suffix, *ji*, to his name. Because of the esteem in which Gandhi was held, people now addressed him as *Gandhiji*.

"Gandhiji," one of the ashram dwellers said to him

one day, "a young couple whom I know and whom I consider wonderful people would like to join our farm. There is only one problem—they are outcastes."

Gandhi, as an orthodox Hindu, believed in the caste system which he thought was a shield of the weak against the strong. Yet he drew a sharp line between religion and discrimination. So he said to the man, "Tell them to come to live with us. There is no objection to them at all."

The couple joined the group and became most useful members of the ashram.

This event brought Gandhi face to face with an ancient problem of his native land. While it was true that the caste system was built into the Hindu creed, one did not have to accept all the traditions passed down to posterity. Times had changed and people's approach to social problems had to change, too. Christians had had their Reformation, and there was no reason, Gandhi thought, why the Hindus should not have a reformation of their own. Before India was set to rule itself, it had to do away with this vestige of the past. Many Indians wanted Gandhi to lead the way to a better future. He saw his first task as cleansing them of their prejudices against the untouchables. He called together his followers in the ashram and told them that the *pariahs*, as the untouchables were also called, stood closer to God than members of other castes because they suffered more. He gave the outcastes a new status, and called them *Harijans*, the children of God.

Gandhi's ashram in India was to have a great mission—
to spread the teaching that the Harijans were worthy
members of the Indian society. His first retreat near Durban had been called Phoenix Farm after the mythical
bird, and the second retreat had been called Tolstoi
Farm after the Russian writer. What was to be the name
of the third Indian ashram? Gandhi decided promptly—
he called it Satyagraha Ashram, devoted to the idea of
fighting for freedom peacefully, including freedom from
discrimination for the children of God. For two years the
retreat stood at its original site, and then it was transferred to another location in the Ahmadabad area, on
the banks of the Sabarmati River.

Meanwhile war engulfed Europe and spread to Asia,
too. The British represented themselves as the champions
of freedom and fighters of tyranny. If that was so, why
did they not relax their hold on India? While the war
continued, the time seemed right to remind the British
that there was also an Indian problem. And Gandhi *did*
remind them, in a speech at the opening of the Hindu
Central College University at Benares, on February 6,
1916. In that address, he opened up new vistas for India.

"If we are to have self-government," he told his people, "we have to take it." These were strong words which
gave new goals to his satyagraha campaign.

Gandhi spoke boldly because his ears were attuned to
great changes in the world. The President of the United
States spoke on behalf of his nation and called upon the
Allies "to make the world safe for democracy." In 1917,

Russia became Communist, and one of its avowed aims was to "make the world safe from colonialism."

After four agonizing years, the Allies won the war. Was the rule of democracy to be extended to India, too? In preparation for changes, the British secretary of state for India and the viceroy drew up a proposal known as the Montagu-Chelmsford Report, to serve as the foundation of the British India Act of 1919. It stated that Britain's policy was to "provide for the increasing association of Indians in every branch of administration and the gradual development of self-governing institutions with a view to the progressive realization of responsible government in British India as an integral part of the British Empire."

"Laudable intentions," Gandhi commented, "but how will they be carried out?"

The execution of the plan disappointed him and the people of India. This was not "making the world safe for democracy." The Federal Legislative Assembly in New Delhi, the capital of British India, was allowed only advisory functions. Just about one million Indians were given the right to vote for the "advisers."

Popular indignation erupted throughout the country. The British countered by enacting dictatorial laws. People charged with hostile acts toward the government could be jailed without trial.

These measures, known as the "Rowlatt acts," infuriated the people of India, and their resentment was particularly strong in the city of Amritsar in the Punjab

Province. A protest meeting was called there for April 13, 1919, to be held in a public park known as Jallianwala Bagh, which was surrounded by high walls and had only a few narrow exit lanes. Thousands of people gathered to voice their protest. General Reginald Dyer, the British military commander of the region, led his soldiers to the meeting place. Prior to the meeting, he had issued orders for Indians to crawl on all fours in a part of town where they had allegedly insulted an English lady.

The general's park platoon consisted of fifty soldiers. Without giving the assemblage a chance to disperse, he ordered his men to fire into the crowd. The shooting continued until all the ammunition was gone. Then the casualties were counted; more than four hundred people had been killed. Dyer was so satisfied with the results that he reported to London that the "targets had been good." Die-hard Europeans hailed the general as the "savior of the Punjab," and presented him with a decorative sword.

News of the "Amritsar massacre" spread to all parts of India, and this event became a turning point in Gandhi's life. Until then he had criticized British rule mildly, but now he denounced it as "satanic." After the massacre he could not sleep for days, meditating on what to do. Then one night he had an inspiration.

"The idea of *hartal* came to me," he confided to his followers. Hartal was the complete cesssation of every public activity. He called on the people to shun British-run courts and schools, setting up their own substitutes.

Also, they should boycott all other English authorities and act in a way to make the continued stay of their rulers completely unprofitable. It should be the patriotic duty of every Indian household to acquire a spinning wheel, make homespun cloth and turn it into the dhoti, while women should wear the saris that they themselves made. The spinning wheel and the dhoti now became symbols of Indian nationalism.

Gandhi knew that the lifeblood of every movement is organization. He decided to turn the Indian National Congress, which had been in existence now for several decades, into the framework of a nationalist movement. Until then it had been the organization of the higher social classes, but now it would be an organization of the masses. Gandhi changed the Congress from a talking shop into a militant organization. Jawaharlal Nehru, who would become free India's first prime minister and who became Gandhi's number one disciple, said this about the startling change:

"Gandhi was like a powerful current of fresh air that made us stretch ourselves and take deep breaths! Like a beam of light that pierced the darkness and removed the scales from our eyes; like a whirlwind that upset many things but most of all the working peoples' minds. He did not descend from the top but seemed to emerge from the millions of India, speaking their language and incessantly drawing attention to them and their appalling condition. 'Get off the backs of these peasants and workers,' he told us, 'all you who live by their exploitation; get rid of the system that produces poverty and misery.' "

An organization was, of course, essential to the success of Gandhi's work. But he also had to have a press organ in which he could "think aloud." He launched a militant weekly—*Young India* in English; *Navajivan* in Gujarati—in which he strongly underscored the work of the Congress. "We are challenging the might of the British government," he wrote in the September 16, 1921, issue of *Young India*, "because we consider its activity wholly evil."

"How can there be any compromise," he asked on February 23, 1922, "whilst the British lion continues to shake its gory claws in our face?"

These were strong words. The government charged him with sedition, had him arrested, and tried him in Ahmadabad. He pleaded guilty.

"I am innocent, of course, of sedition," he said, "but I don't want to contest the charge. I believe in ahimsa, no violence, even in such matters."

Justice C. N. Broomfield was the presiding judge.

"Mr. Gandhi," he said, "the law is no respecter of persons. Nevertheless, it will be impossible to ignore the fact that you are in a different category from any person I have ever tried. . . . It would be impossible to ignore the fact that in the eyes of millions of your countrymen you are a great patriot and a great leader. Even those who differ from you in politics look upon you as a man of high ideals and of noble and even saintly life. . . . I should like to say in sentencing you that if the course of events in India should make it possible for the government to reduce the period and release you, no one will be better pleased than I."

After this pronouncement, the judge sentenced Gandhi to six years in jail. The convicted prisoner now asked Judge Broomfield to permit him to say a few words.

"As far as the sentence is concerned," Gandhi said, "I certainly consider it as light as any judge could inflict upon me, and as far as the proceedings are concerned, I must say that I could not have expected greater courtesy." He was sentenced in March, 1922. According to the Indian standards of that time, he was an old man, fifty-three. Would he be able to survive six years in jail?

Gandhi was transported to Yeravda Central Prison near the city of Poona in the Central Division of the Province of Bombay. Not only did he survive his stay in prison, but he was to survive many more terms. In the course of time, Yeravda prison became his second home.

The day that Gandhi entered his cell, it was filled with flowers, and messages of admiration reached him from all over India. He could not have received a grander welcome if he had been a powerful prince.

The letters and telegrams continued to flood into his prison. Countless people asked his advice, prayed for his health and welfare, and offered him their help. The warden and guards treated their prisoner with deep respect.

Soon his cell began to look more like an editorial office than a jail. He also found several assistants among the younger political prisoners.

Before his jail sentence, Gandhi had been urged to write his autobiography and also of his experiences in South Africa. He had been too busy to find the time and he was not a fluent writer. Also, he claimed that there were incidents in his life that filled his heart with shame. But now he had the time to meditate, remember, and write. In Yeravda jail, Gandhi wrote *Satyagraha in South Africa*, and there he began his autobiography, *The Story of My Experiments with Truth*.

In his recollections, he wrote frankly about his youth and about his many troubles. He was in the midst of his work when he was taken ill. The doctors diagnosed it as appendicitis.

Gandhi had to undergo surgery immediately. An appendix operation was not as safe at that time as it is today, and Gandhi was an "old" man with limited reserves of strength. The British authorities were concerned. What would happen if their prisoner were to die during surgery? The government might be accused of causing his death, which could touch off a campaign of violence. The English thought it wiser to release him from jail. In February, 1924, Gandhi was free again, having served less than one third of his term. He underwent surgery and recovered quickly. Although he looked feeble, he was really very strong.

In his ashram at Sabarmati, Gandhi continued to attend to his daily routine. During the summer following his release, there was a particularly violent eruption of religious hatred among the Hindus and Muslims in parts of India. Although the Hindus were a majority in the country, the ancestors of the Muslims had ruled India for centuries. How could the nation be free of British rule if it could not keep peace between its two largest communities? In this critical situation, India's eyes were on Gandhi. Could he stop the communal riots? He moved quickly, trying persuasion in his publications, but it was no use. Then he made a startling decision. He decided to stop eating, and he would "fast unto death" until the riots stopped. He began his fast unto death in the Delhi house of Mohammed Ali, a Muslim friend.

Taking slight refreshments, Gandhi continued his "Great Fast" for twenty-one days. There were many riot casualties, but people at last began to heed his resolve. Also, the rioters became exhausted, and the English applied strong measures.

At the end of this critical year, in December, 1924, Gandhi was asked to assume the presidency of the Indian National Congress. He did this at the annual meeting in Belgaum, in the Southern Division of Bombay. He served faithfully for the usual term of one year, but this work did not appeal to him. As head of the Congress party he was subject to pressures and found himself in the midst of political operations. He was at his best when giving advice, not directives. As an adviser he was unique; as a political figure he was less effective.

Meanwhile, young people arose within the Congress party, more impatient than Gandhi. One of them was Dr. Bhimrao Ramji Ambedkar, an untouchable. Jealous of Gandhi, Ambedkar attacked him as a man too deeply steeped in Indian lore. He insisted that Gandhi belonged to another age. Gandhi believed in what he said were the better features of the caste system, which Ambedkar considered India's shame. At the same time, Ambedkar said, Gandhi claimed to be against untouchability. But anyone who accepted the caste system had to accept the condition of the untouchables. Gandhi pointed to his work on behalf of the children of God. Ambedkar re-mained unimpressed.

"Gandhiji is getting old," some of the Congress party members said. "India needs industries, and he wants to take us back to the spinning wheel. What kind of country will we be if we must wear the dhoti? What is going to happen to our infant textile industry? Gandhi wants to rush us back into the seventeenth century on the grounds that it was our golden age. How golden was an age in which life was the cheapest commodity in India?"

"Satyagraha?" others grumbled. "How naive can you be? Did the Irish gain their independence by nonvio-lence? And what about the Poles and the Czechs? You must fight for freedom and independence! India should not wait for the British to grant us favors because of Gandhi's saintliness."

At the annual party session at Cawnpore in December, 1925, more voices were raised against Gandhi's moderate policy. Gandhi spoke at that session, taking notice of the attacks against him. He said that he believed his approach to India's problem was right, but he did not want to force it upon others. Infallibility was a trait he never claimed for himself. India was a very complicated country and its problems had countless ramifications. He wanted to think about many of these problems and for that he needed time. For a year, he said, he was not going to express his opinion on public issues. He would study and meditate.

During this time Gandhi still saw to the needs of the Sabarmati ashram dwellers, traveled about the country, and kept his fingers on the pulse of India. In spite of the criticism leveled against him by Congress members, his reputation as the conscience of the subcontinent remained undimmed. He had helped to make the British realize that there was an "Indian problem," and that for a democracy such as Britain to rule India was a contradiction of its principles. Some way should be found to give the people greater say in the determination of their fates. The first step had to be an inquiry into the condition of India; the second step was to recommend reforms. The British took these steps, and a parliamentary commission was set up in November, 1927, under the chairmanship of Sir John Simon, a respected leader of the Liberal party.

Indian leaders were not impressed by the commission because it had only English members; not one single Indian. The commission traveled to India, held hearings, and studied a vast collection of documents. It all took time, a very long time, and Congress party leaders were dismayed by the delay. "This is a typical British stalling operation," they said. There had been too many inquiries into the condition of India. The subcontinent needed quick action.

To Gandhi, as he surveyed the political scene, it made no sense that Britain should rule over a population nearly ten times the size of its own. The subcontinent should be the homeland of its people, and not for the English to use as an instrument of their imperial aims. India should become the end and not merely the means. Gandhiji decided to share the results of his thinking with his people, and he did that at the Calcutta session of the Indian National Congress party in December, 1928. He presented the English with an ultimatum.

"Long enough have we been your servants and you our masters. We now call upon you to turn over the government of our country to us. We do not ask that this be done today. We know that it takes time to transfer power. We have to prepare ourselves for it, too, and one year should be enough for that purpose. Listen therefore to us: one year from now we expect our roles to be reversed. We shall be the masters and you may serve us if you wish. We want independence by December, 1929. Should you fail to live up to your obligation, we shall use our most effective weapon against you. You know, of course, that it will not be violence, in which we do not believe. It is to be satyagraha, nonviolent disobedience to your laws. It will not be a spotty piecemeal affair, but an all-Indian satyagraha. We expect that it will paralyze the operation of your unjust regime."

"Independence within a year," the Congress party echoed.

"Independence within a year," millions of Indians repeated.

Gandhi's announcement of his decision was a historic occasion. Everybody knew now that he, and he alone, was the conscience of India and that he alone spoke for its hundreds of millions. His people would have given him any of the honored titles by which Indians respect their great men; *guru*, the teacher, or *gurudev*, the great teacher, or *pandit*, the scholar. But the people of India reserved a name for Gandhi that was not conferred on anyone else. It was suggested by India's greatest poet, Rabindranath Tagore. The Nobel Prize-winning writer began to call Gandhi the *Mahatma*, the Great Soul, and he became known by that name at home and abroad.

Months passed, and the work of Sir John Simon's commission was still far from completed. No change in the status of the subcontinent could be expected before its termination. Would Britain hold on to its prey forever? Gandhi wondered.

The next annual session of the Congress party took place in the city of Lahore. One full year had elapsed since Gandhi's announcement. The time had come for the people of India to act. The Congress spoke on their behalf in December, 1929, and the word it said was "Independence." It designated January 26, 1930, as National Independence Day.

This was, of course, a one-sided declaration which the British had no intention of carrying out. The Congress party therefore decided to follow Gandhi's advice and proclaim a nationwide satyagraha. Patriotic Indians were expected to boycott all the British government organs, including the courts and schools. They were not to buy foreign cloth, but would use products of their handicrafts.

It was up to the "conscience of India," to the Great Soul, to dramatize the Congress party's decision of satyagraha, the nonviolent civil disobedience. And Gandhi dramatized it in such a way that it was to become known even in the most distant Himalayan hamlets. The dramatization assumed the shape of the Great Salt March.

6

The Great Salt March and Its Sequel

Salt is a product that even the poorest people need, and it was a product on which the British had placed a tax. Mahatma Gandhi decided to dramatize satyagraha by inducing his people to refuse to buy salt. The salt industry was a government monopoly, and its price included the tax.

Gandhi also decided to make salt, which was against the law. He could have done this by going to the shore and taking a pinch of salt out of the sea water. However, Mohandas Gandhi was not only the Great Soul, but he was also a great showman. His showmanship served a noble cause—the interests of his people. Showmanship required that ample time be given for the people to take notice of his act of defiance. It required build-up, background, maximum publicity, the climactic moment for

the flashlights, the film cameras, the newspaper corre-
spondents clamoring for statements, interviews, and an
atmosphere of excitement. Gandhi's Great Salt March
would show the showmen and the statesmen of the world
how a small Indian could become a giant.

Gandhi did not go to the seashore by train or car to
make the salt—a distance he then would have covered in
a matter of hours. Instead, he decided to walk. It would
now take him twenty-four days, and cause the tension to
rise to a tremendous climax. First, however, he gave warning to the British.

The highest British official in India was Lord Irwin,
the viceroy, later Earl of Halifax. Gandhi addressed a
letter to him, asking that the salt tax be repealed.

"If my letter makes no appeal to your heart," Gandhi
wrote, "on the eleventh day of this month, I shall proceed with such workers of the ashram as I can take, to
disregard the provisions of the salt tax. I regard this tax
as the most iniquitous from the poor man's standpoint.
As the independence movement is for the poorest of the
land, the beginning will be made with this evil."

The viceroy ignored the Great Soul. It was his secretary who replied. "His Excellency . . . regrets to learn
that you contemplate a course of action which is clearly
bound to involve violation of the law and danger to public peace."

Gandhi gave the signal for the salt march to the sea,
two hundred miles away. He would walk that distance to

make a pinch of salt. Seventy-nine people from his retreat began the march with him on March 12, 1930.

The night before, countless people wearing hand-spun cloth had begun streaming toward Gandhi's ashram at Sabarmati to witness the beginning of what appeared to be a historic march.

"The scenes that preceded, accompanied, and followed this great national event were so enthusiastic, magnificent, and soul-stirring," the *Bombay Chronicle* reported, "that they, indeed, beggar description. Never was the wave of patriotism so powerful in the hearts of mankind as it was on this great occasion which is bound to go down in the chapters of history of India's national freedom as a great beginning of a great movement."

Ahmadabad was the first city that the procession reached. Hundreds and then thousands joined the marchers as they proceeded westward. A tremendous outpouring of people flanked the procession along the country lanes, on the roofs of huts, and from the tops of trees. Gandhi, now past sixty, marched at the head of the snaking column, striding with long steps, a stick in his firm grip. He looked more owlish than ever, his spectacles riding the tip of his nose, a smile on his face. Everywhere he went the air resounded with the thunderous shout: "*Gandhi ki-jai*" (Victory to Gandhi). He was the leader of a vast army moving into battle for a great cause.

The procession reached the sea on April 6, at the town of Dandi. There the press, film operators, and radio commentators were ready for the historic scene.

At exactly six in the morning, Gandhi proceeded to the seashore, walking slowly, with grave solemnity. On the shore he stopped and said his prayers. Here and there were deposits of salt left by the sea. Gandhi picked up a pinch of salt and held it on his outstretched palm as the movie cameras whirred. "God be praised," he said," for this happy ending of the first stage of our final struggle for freedom."

Then, through the reporters, he addressed his words to all of India.

"Now that the ceremonial breach of the salt law has been consummated, it is open to all who would take the risk of legal prosecution to manufacture salt. My advice is that people should do so everywhere, and instruct fellow villagers in how to do it, while telling them of the risk. It should be made absolutely clear that this breach of an unjust law is done in the open and is in no way stealthy."

The salt which Gandhi had picked up was "sold" to the highest bidder at a public auction, the proceeds to go to the Congress party campaign funds. The purchase price was sixteen hundred *rupees*, representing hundreds of dollars.

An unarmed insurrection against the colonial authority followed. Villagers along India's vast coast waded into the sea with pans to make the tax-free salt. The police reacted with mass arrests, and Ramdas, Gandhi's third son, was one of the prisoners. As violation of the salt law spread, the police began to use force. The lawbreakers never resisted arrest, but they did resist the confiscation of their salt. Police raided the Congress party headquarters in Bombay where salt was being produced in pans on the building roof. A crowd of sixty thousand assembled. Hundreds of them were handcuffed, their arms tied with ropes, and they were marched off to jail.

Gandhi's favorite disciple, Jawaharlal Nehru, recorded these events: "It seemed as though a spring had suddenly released all over the country, in town and village; salt manufacture was the topic of the day. . . . As we saw the abounding enthusiasm of the people and the way saltmaking was spreading like a prairie fire, we felt a little abashed for having questioned the efficacy of this method when it was first proposed by Gandhiji. And we marveled at the amazing knack of the man to impress the multitude to make it act in an organized way."

Gandhi set up a temporary ashram at Camp Karadi, a mango grove between Dandi and the sea, from where he kept in close contact with developments throughout the land.

Until this time, the police had not interfered with Gandhi's activities. But they did act on May 5. At forty-five minutes past midnight, Gandhi was awakened in his camp by the tramping of feet. The district superintendent, heading a police detachment of thirty men from a nearby town, was looking for Gandhi. Shaken awake, it took Gandhi several seconds to realize what was happening.

"Have you come to arrest me?" he asked the superintendent softly.

"Yes," the man answered, "if your name is Mohandas Karamchand Gandhi."

"Do you mind waiting a bit until I wash my face?" The policeman said that he did not mind.

By that time the camp was wide awake, and the members of the ashram asked Gandhi, "*Bapu*, let us sing your favorite *bhajan* (hymn)."

Gandhi led the singing in his reedy voice. Then he was ready to go.

The arresting officer had to take his prisoner to the nearest stop of the night mail-express to Bombay, and he was in a hurry.

Gandhi took along a small bundle of bedding and a satchel.

"*Bapu*," his followers asked, "what is your message for Kasturbai?"

"Tell her that she is a brave woman and that she may lose her husband for many years."

The convoy was on its way. Gandhi was delivered into the keeping of the warden of Yeravda prison, his "second home." Again the prison officials greeted him like old friends. Nobody knew how long he was going to be their "guest." This time he was not placed on trial, but would stay in prison under special ordinances "at the pleasure of His Majesty." In reality, it was the "pleasure" of the British officials in India.

The next session of the Indian Congress party took place in December. This time there was no quorum present because the leaders were in jail. One hundred thousand persons had been arrested in the wake of the great salt march, while the campaign of civil disobedience continued. India was truly a boiling caldron.

Again Gandhi's cell in Yeravda jail became more a business executive's office than a place of detention for a political prisoner. An extra cell was placed at his disposal for two secretaries, and he was also given a conference room. He read his mail, dictated letters, engaged in political talks, mapped out strategy, and sent messages to influential people in England.

The head of the British government was now Ramsay MacDonald, leader of the Labor party, a man who had come from the laboring classes himself. Labor seemed more sympathetic to the Indian cause than had the conservatives. India was Britain's "unfinished business." London held that some action had to be taken to put an end to satyagraha, which threatened to immobilize the government.

Deputies of Viceroy Irwin were frequent visitors to Gandhi's cell. They treated him as a negotiating partner, not a prisoner. Meanwhile, the prime minister in London was preparing a conference on Indian affairs, at which representatives of the subcontinent were to speak as equal partners. It was to be a "round table conference": nobody would sit at the head of the table. Would Gandhi accept the viceroy's invitation to attend?

Before the meeting, agreement had to be reached to end the civil disobedience campaign. The viceroy tried to show that it was hurting the people of India no less than the British. Business was slowing down, reaching almost a standstill, and people were thrown out of work. So it was decided that before the conference, Gandhi and the viceroy must have a meeting of their own.

Prisoner Gandhi did not readily consent to sit down at the same table with the mighty viceroy. First he consulted his fellow prisoners, some of whom had held high office in the Congress party. He also consulted other leading Indians and asked the advice of British friends. As a result of these consultations, he expressed his willingness to listen to the viceroy. The Yeravda prisoner carried on the negotiations with the viceroy as an equal. The meeting resulted in an agreement, and Gandhi was ready to be India's spokesman at the conference.

On a January day in 1931, word was sent to the warden of Yeravda jail to release Gandhi and thirty other Congress party leaders. There was, however, no farewell party because, as Gandhi jokingly told the warden, he had a feeling that soon he might be back.

From the jail, the Mahatma proceeded to the viceroy's residence where he was welcomed with much ceremony. The press photographers were again on hand. Viceroy Irwin was a towering person, representing the majesty of a government whose power extended around the globe. Next to him stood the frail, owl-like little Indian, his broad grin revealing the stumps of his teeth. He was clad in his dhoti, and yet he conveyed an inner majesty.

Occasionally, Gandhi did look like a meek little man, but he was far from that. In later years, Lord Irwin revealed that in all his diplomatic career he had never met a tougher opponent. It took weeks before the two men agreed on the wording of the document which was preliminary to the Round Table Conference held in London to discuss the Indian question. Finally, in March, 1931, the Delhi Pact was ready for the signatures of the viceroy and of Gandhi. It temporarily called an end to civil disobedience.

After the signatures were affixed, Lord Irwin invited Gandhi to tea, the "strongest" beverage the Mahatma ever drank.

"I will be glad to have tea with you," he said with his impish smile, "but I always spice it, and put a pinch of this illegal salt into my cup to remind us of our New Delhi Tea Party." The viceroy smiled.

In August, Gandhi was again at the great gateway city of India, ready to sail to England for the Round Table Conference. He was accompanied by three secretary-associates: Mahadev Desai, for twenty-four years his secretary and chronicler; Sarojini Naidu, poetess, Indian nationalist leader, and former president of the Congress party; and Madeleine Slade, daughter of a British admiral.

There was a large crowd on the pier to see the little man embark on the HMS *Rajputana*. The ship was filled with dignitaries headed for the conferences; British advisers, Indian princes, and their retinue. But the crowd on the pier was not interested in them. All eyes were focused on the Mahatma.

His admirers were on hand, too, when his ship stopped at Aden. The leading statesman of Egypt, Nahas Pasha, went on board to greet Gandhi when the *Rajputana* made a coaling stop at Suez. A still larger crowd greeted him when the boat docked at the French port of Marseilles. Finally, the ship arrived in London.

On his first arrival in England, Gandhi had worn typical English flannels. This time, however, he wore only his dhoti, the loincloth which had become his trademark.

"What a showman," the leading commentator of one of Britain's best-known weeklies, *The Spectator*, remarked. "The man in the dhoti is the most photogenic person in the world today."

Gandhi had invitations to live in mansions during his stay in London, but decided to make his home at Kingsley House, a social settlement in the slums. He also maintained a temporary office in Knightsbridge, near the conference headquarters in St. James' Palace. He was "Uncle Gandhi" to the slum children, and crowds followed him everywhere. "Mr. Gandhi is the best news value in the world," a London daily wrote.

Gandhi met some of the famous names of England, including George Bernard Shaw and the movie comedian, Charlie Chaplin. Mr. Shaw, who always thought highly of himself, said of Gandhi, "The Mahatma is the type of man that comes once in a thousand years." At a meeting with Chaplin, it was Gandhi who kept the great comedian in stitches with his wry humor. General Smuts called on Gandhi, too, and, referring to their South African differences, told him, "I did not give you such a bad time as you gave me."

Gandhi received an invitation to the royal residence in Buckingham Palace to have tea with King George V. He was a unique sight in those august quarters as he turned up in his dhoti.

Twenty-four hours a day were not enough for Gandhi during his London stay. This was a typical day: 1:00 A.M. he reached his Kingsley Hall room; 1:45, finished his spinning quota of one hundred and sixty yards of yarn; 1:50, wrote the diary of the previous day; 2:00 to 3:35 he slept; 3:45, washed and prayed; 5:00 to 6:00, rested; 6:00 to 7:00 he walked and gave interviews surrounded by journalists; 7:00 to 8:00 he performed his morning bath; 8:00 to 8:30 he breakfasted; 8:30 to 9:15, made the trip to his office; 9:15 to 10:45, gave interviews; 10:45 to 11:00, journeyed to St. James' Palace; 11:00 A.M. to 1:00 P.M., participated in the Round Table Conference; 1:00 to 2:45, addressed American journalists at a luncheon meeting; 3:00 to 5:30, conferred with Muslims; 5:00 to 7:00, conferred with the secretary of state for India; 7:00 to 7:30, was back in Kingsley Hall for meal and prayers; 8:00 to 9:10, talked with temperance workers; 9:10 to 9:45, conferred with the Nawah of Bhopal, a Muslim prince; 12:30, returned to Kingsley Hall for an hour and a half of sleep.

Gandhi took part in special programs on certain days. Two days after his arrival, on September 13, he spoke over an American radio network to people in the United States, and this was a new experience for him. When shown the microphone in the radio studio he asked curiously, "Do I have to speak into this thing?"

By that time he was on the air, and those were his first words America heard. He summarized the philosophy of his life in the radio speech.

"Only by attaining freedom can India revive the glories of its ancient past," he insisted.

After making that clear, he also made a special point. Freedom would help not only India but the rest of the world as well. Indians would be better off and able to use the goods that America produced. Then he reverted to his constant theme: "Neither violence nor conventional diplomacy are our methods. Our weapons are truth and nonviolence. I would rather wait than gain our freedom by violent means now."

Gandhi was given a sign that his time for the American broadcast was drawing to its end. With a deep sigh, he brought his talk to a close.

"Well, that was that." He was still on the air, and those were the last words that his American audience heard.

In the midst of all this activity, Gandhi had to concentrate on the object of his visit—the Round Table Conference, designed to frame an Indian constitution with broader rights for the subcontinent. The round table around which the participants sat must have been gigantic indeed, because there were one hundred and twelve delegates. They represented the Congress party, as well as the Muslim League, the latter having been in existence for a quarter of a century as the spokesman of Muslims on the subcontinent. Present also were delegates of more than five hundred native princes and, of course, of the British administration, operating through the I. C. S., Indian Civil Service. The chief representative of Britain was the lord chancellor, John Sankey.

But round table or not, the "head of the table" was wherever the Mahatma sat.

The problems which the conference faced were overpowering. Not only did the relations between the British and the Indians have to be settled, but also relations between the Indians themselves, and between British India, ruled directly from London, and the India of the Princes, where British rule was indirect.

Since the eyes of the world were focused on Gandhi, it is of interest to see what impression he gave at this historic London stay. Newspaper reporters and other observers all over the world paid close attention to him. The most perceptive description was given by Harold Laski, the English social scientist, who wrote about Gandhi's part in the conference to his friend, Oliver Wendell Holmes, Jr., justice of the United States Supreme Court.

"Gandhi is really remarkable," the English scholar wrote, "and there is no difficulty in understanding the veneration which he inspires. He is quiet, precise, subtle, and there is an inner dignity about him, which is of supreme quality."

Gandhi did not speak with eloquence in a strong resonant voice, but he made his points crystal-clear. He employed the simplest words—"Biblical simplicity," an observer noted—when he spoke in his high-pitched, nasal voice.

His greatness comes, Laski thought, "from what the Quakers call the inner light, the power of internal self-confidence which, having established its principles, is completely impervious to reason."

In a memorable speech at the end of the conference, Gandhi summarized the Congress' views:

"Call it by any name you like, a rose will smell as sweet by any other name, but it must be the rose of liberty I want, not an artificial product. . . . I don't want to break the bond between England and India but I do want to transform it. I want to transform slavery into complete freedom for my land. . . ."

The last word was said and now it was up to the British to act. The problem they faced was difficult. It seemed there were too many divisions in India to be reconciled— between the Hindus and the Muslims; the caste people and the "scheduled castes"; British India and the India of the Princes. But eventually the British did present their plan. Elections were to take place, but they would not be on a national level. Special electorates were proposed for the Hindus, the Muslims, for the scheduled castes, and for princely India. There was not one word about independence for India, either within or without the British Commonwealth.

"The old imperialist game," the Congress party leaders commented sadly. "The more groups they set up, the more pawns they can employ in their game. This is the same old story of divide and rule. It is totally unacceptable to us."

A disappointed Gandhi took the ship to India. British newspapers were saddened, too, having lost their "most colorful character." On his way home, Gandhi stopped off in Switzerland and Italy, meeting famous writers and statesmen. Finally, he embarked on the long voyage home. His ship docked in Bombay on December 28, 1931.

"Even though I have come home empty handed," he told interviewers, "I have not compromised India's honor."

Shortly after his return, the annual session of the Congress party met, and authorized renewal of the satyagraha, the fourth great national effort of noncooperation with the British authorities.

In retaliation for this act, Gandhi was taken into custody on January 4, 1932, and some thirty thousand others were rounded up and shipped off to jail. They were arrested under a century-old regulation which made no provision for trial or for a fixed term of imprisonment.

"From Buckingham Palace to jail," Gandhi quipped when he showed up at the gate of the prison.

The warden of Yeravda prison welcomed his distinguished prisoner, assigned him to his old cell, and gave adjacent cells to his secretaries and friends. Gandhi was "home" again.

7

The Epic Fast and Its Aftermath

Gandhi had rejected the British plan of reform as inadequate. Yet London went ahead with its schedule for introducing changes such as the proposed elections in the provinces. The untouchables, whom Gandhi had named the Harijans, were to have their own electorates. The leader of the untouchables, Dr. Ambedkar, who occupied a prominent position in the Congress party, wanted separate elections since he feared that otherwise his people would be swamped in elections by the caste Hindus.

However, Gandhi was against a special election for the Harijans. In his view, it represented discrimination against them. The British ignored his objections and proceeded with their plans. Gandhi decided to take a determined stand. He had only one weapon at his disposal in jail—starving himself to death. All the world now respected the saintly man, and the British could not afford to have his death on their conscience. Yet the British Empire could not retreat in the face of opposition from a "wilful old man." Besides, the authorities thought that Gandhi would change his mind at the last moment.

Gandhi did not change his mind. He was to begin his fast on September 20, 1932. On the appointed day, he rose in the early hours as usual, and prepared himself for the ordeal by having his favorite *Vaishnava Jana* hymn sung at morning prayers. Its haunting refrain was "He alone is the true Vaishnava [Supreme God], who knows and feels the people's woes." Gandhi then took his customary meal of fruit and milk, while a companion recited a passage from the *Gita*. In midmorning he took his last meal of lemon juice and honey mixed with hot water. A minute later the jail bell struck twelve, and with its last stroke Gandhi's "epic fast" began.

Now the cell in Yeravda prison was transformed into a stage upon which the eyes of the world rested. Swarms of reporters and photographers surrounded the walls, awaiting the outcome of the fast. They also wanted to catch glimpses of the friends and admirers arriving in constant streams, imploring Gandhi to break his fast. A king could not have commanded more attention than the little brown man in the cell.

Gandhi continued his fast. His eyes sank deeper into his face and his frail body grew thinner. Wires buzzed all over the world, carrying bulletins about the condition of the prisoner in Yeravda jail.

Jawaharlal Nehru, then a top leader in the Congress

party and an ardent fighter for Indian independence, said, "What a magician is this little man, and how well he knows to pull the strings that move peoples' hearts."

The issue was clear. Gandhi made it clear in countless statements that he wanted no special electoral status for the Harijans. The final decision, he said, was up to the government. The heart of the government was at 10 Downing Street in London, the prime minister's residence. There, the weakening condition of the prisoner in Yeravda kept the high officials in tense conferences as they listened to the latest bulletins about the fast.

Gandhi was rigid in his demands. "No compromise, please; the solution should be clear-cut. We cannot accept a separate electoral arrangement for the children of God, since that would perpetuate the baneful spirit of discrimination that lies heavy on the land." But the British government was committed to its solution and could not withdraw without losing face.

Meanwhile people prayed for the survival of the Great Soul in hundreds of thousands of villages and towns. To induce him to break his fast, some caste Hindus opened their shrines and wells to the untouchables for the first time in Indian history. Gandhi's answer was, "No compromise."

Gandhi had been fasting now for five days, and the reserves of energy in his frail body were running low. Physicians attending him passed the word that his end was near. Even younger men could not have lasted much longer.

Faced with the possibility of Gandhi's death, emergency meetings were held in the palace in New Delhi and at 10 Downing Street. The sixth day of the fast dawned—might this be Gandhi's last? All night, long-distance telephone conversations and urgent wires had been exchanged. At last a decision was made. The viceroy yielded, the British Empire yielded, and so did the leader of the untouchables, Dr. Ambedkar. Britain was ready to give up its plan for a special scheduled-castes election in India.

After the decision had been reached, the British imperial representative rushed into Gandhi's cell. He found Gandhi in the company of Rabindranath Tagore, the poet. Gandhi was informed of the government's decision and he was now ready to break his fast. Propped up in his bed, he signed the "Yeravda Pact."

"After the fast, untouchability forfeited its public approval," the American writer Louis Fischer commented. "It had been socially improper to consort with the Harijans. In many circles, it now became socially improper not to consort with them."

An upsurge of sentiment against discrimination swept the land. Caste Hindus went out of their way to fraternize with the "children of God" in public. In Allahabad alone, twelve caste-temples were opened to them. Entire states, such as Kashmir, Baroda, Kolhapur, and Bhor, banned discrimination. Even some of the most tradition-bound shrines were thrown open to the outcastes, as for instance, the Kaligat Temple in Calcutta and the Ram Mandier in Benares, the holiest Indian town.

But for Gandhi this was only the beginning. He feared that the emotional upsurge would soon yield to past practices, and that spelled discrimination. Even though the Yeravda Pact stated that "no one shall be regarded as untouchable by reason of birth," old habits, he found, could not be erased merely by signing a document.

In 1933, Gandhi began another fast designed to end the ban against the Harijans' admission to all caste shrines. This brought about his unconditional release from prison. However, before the year was up he was back in jail for civil disobedience acts. Once more he started to fast, and the government again released him. In 1934, Gandhi retired as president of the Congress party.

Gandhi decided to teach his countrymen to turn their backs forever on discrimination. He transformed his weekly *Young India* into a periodical dedicated to the solution of this problem, and renamed it *Harijan*. He transformed the Sabarmati ashram into a workshop for the dissemination of information against the curse of untouchability.

Now Gandhi undertook a great tour of India, visiting every province, carrying on the campaign against untouchability. Also he wanted to see all of India so he could become better acquainted with its countless faces. As it turned out, India wanted to see him, too.

He traveled for ten months. These months revealed more of the Indian attitude toward Gandhi than had any previous period. During much of Gandhi's travel he was accompanied by Nehru, the man who was now closest to him and who was destined to carry out the policies of the Great Soul.

India came to know Jawaharlal Nehru as *Pandit*, the scholar, and even more as *Panditji*. By birth and education, Nehru was an aristocrat of aristocrats. Born November 14, 1889, he came from the highest Brahman caste, from the lovely land of Kashmir, "nearest to the gods" because of its soaring mountain peaks. He had been educated in the best English schools, graduating from Oxford University in 1910. He was admitted to the bar in 1912. His father, Motilal Nehru, had been a prominent attorney and a leader in the Congress party. Nehru was to play the leading role in the party's movement. He would be known as "Mr. India" after Gandhi's death.

Nehru was also a writer of great distinction. His history of India and his autobiography are considered classics. He wrote in English, and also spoke the Hindustani dialect, although he spoke it with a slight foreign accent.

As Gandhi's companion during the ten-month tour through India, Nehru left graphic descriptions of the people's reactions to the Great Soul.

"I accompanied him . . ." Nehru wrote, "and could not help marveling at the vast crowds he attracted. . . . As we motored through the rural areas we would have gatherings of from ten to twenty-five thousand people every few miles." Sometimes Gandhi attracted hundreds of thousands of people.

On a typical day, the twilight hours brought a lessening of the unbearable heat. Thousands of people were on the march to a meeting place where Gandhiji was to speak. They came long distances, across trackless wastes, on sketchy roads, across the jungle, lashed by the monsoon rains or choked by the dust of the trails. They arrived at the meeting, many of them sitting on the ground in the powdery dust or on the soggy soil. They climbed to tree-tops for a better view, or crouched on tops of the huts. Then Gandhi came.

He spoke to the people in his native Gujarati, mixed occasionally with English or words from Hindi. He set forth basic thoughts, expressed in basic language. Christians in the audience saw much resemblance between his speech and the Biblical language.

"I am telling you, weave your own cloth . . ." adding, "because that will foster home industries and make work for the people."

He returned to his favorite theme, the object of his tour.

"There is only one hope for India . . . if the Harijans are accorded decent treatment and discriminations cease."

There was nothing startling in what he said, and it was known well in advance what he would say. Yet people wanted to hear him. Why? Gandhi's speaking engagements were places of pilgrimage, and people went there to purify themselves in the radiance of his words or just to expose themselves to his presence. Indians have a name for this: *darshan*, the blessing quality of the mere presence of a saintly man.

Gandhi's voice was weak and only people in the first rows could hear it. Sometimes he could not be heard at all. Nehru commented, "Gandhiji was very difficult to understand, and sometimes his language was incomprehensible to a modern man. But we felt that we knew him well enough to realize that he was a great and unique man and a glorious leader."

The millions that came to sit at Gandhi's feet knew that, too, although many could not hear what he said and most did not understand the language he spoke. Toward the end of the tour, Gandhi was so exhausted that he could not speak. Millions came just to see him.

He sat in the center of a wooden platform under strong lights, as the twilight darkness surrounded the audience. The crowd extended as far as the eye could see, people arriving constantly, looking for places. Quietly they sat down, looking intently at the Mahatma as they would look at a supreme being. Many of them no more expected him to talk than they would have expected the god Vishnu to address them. They were delighted to look at him, and that alone filled them with happiness. Keeping silent all the time, Gandhi stood up after a while, ready to continue his journey. After that, the vast assemblage went its way, filled with an inner radiance.

But not everyone was carried away by Gandhi's arguments when he spoke. Nehru himself had reservations about the Mahatma's guiding lines. "Why the spinning wheel in the age of automation?" he asked. It was only gradually that Nehru began to see that the spinning wheel was a symbol of the desire of the people of India to be more dependent upon themselves. Finally Nehru reached a conclusion.

"He is not naive, nor a dreamer living in some fantasy of his own creation. He came from Gujarat, the home of hardheaded businessmen, and he has an unrivaled knowledge of the Indian village and the conditions of life prevailing there. It is out of that personal experience that he evolved the program of the spinning wheel."

The ten months' tour was over. Gandhi returned to his work in the Sabarmati ashram, now dedicated to the struggle for the rights of Harijans. But he needed a larger retreat, and soon found it in Wardha, a town of about four thousand, on a prairie-like plain of good soil. It was located in the Central Provinces where the people speak Marathi, another major language of the country. From there, the ashram was moved to a still more suitable location in nearby Segaon, and it was dedicated to the service of all humanity. A few years later, in 1940, Gandhi changed the name and called it Service Town—*Sevagram*.

In this ashram Gandhi drew up the guidelines that contained his basic philosophy, his way of life. Ahimsa was the main rule—no violence under any circumstances. Gandhi believed violence was contrary to decent human conduct even if the opponent had evil designs. He opposed violence even in the interest of one's country. Killing other human beings was not a virtue and not a sign of patriotism.

Celibacy was another rule of the ashram. People there were to live as if dwellers in a monastery. Gandhi had taken a vow of celibacy long before this. Kasturbai had become his beloved companion in the pursuit of a common cause.

Discrimination was prohibited in the ashram, and the children of God were equal members of the community. Gandhi urged all his countrymen to share this attitude.

Fearlessness was another quality which he expected of members of the retreat. Too many Indians feared too many things, Gandhi said. They would best qualify for independence if they were to shed their fears.

Two related vows formed parts of the ashram ground rules, recommended to all India. These were *swadeshi* and *khaddar*, domestic production of goods and, especially, homespun cloth. The ashram dwellers were expected to devote a certain time to the spinning wheel.

Gandhi also recommended that Indians cultivate their own native tongues instead of English. He thought that

Hindi, being the most widespread native language, should occupy the most prominent place.

These guidelines sought to strengthen the relation between religion and government. In Western countries, these are separate concepts, but for India, Gandhi believed that government should contain the highest principles of religious morality. The government must be dedicated to good deeds.

When Gandhi spoke of these beliefs, not only India but all of the world listened. At Sevagram, he spoke from a one-room hut. It was crowded with the tools that he needed for his work, especially the spinning wheel on which he worked several hours every day. His best ideas occurred to him, he said, when working at the wheel.

His room also contained the tools he needed to patch up the roof and fill the holes after a heavy battering by the rains. All types of medicine bottles cluttered his table because many people sought his medical aid.

Gandhi helped in the garden, too. Most of the dwellers tilled the soil, raising their own vegetables, and all of them were on a vegetarian diet. The Mahatma conducted prayer services, and he read his favorite passages of the sacred scripts of several creeds, especially the poetic sections of the *Gita.*

Gandhi's concern for life—any kind of life—was so great that not even a snake was allowed to be killed in his ashram. It was a living creature, he reminded his visitors, anxious to fill out its span of life. He warned his followers not even to frighten such a creature. "If you leave him alone," he said, "he will leave you alone, too."

Of course, Gandhi drank no alcohol and did not smoke. He kept himself fit by walking. He would walk long distances in the gathering dusk, moving with long strides, relishing the breeze after sunset. Some of his disciples followed him, anxious to hear him on many subjects. He answered them earnestly, in short sentences spoken in his simple language. Yet, he liked fun, too, and could tell a joke as well as anybody. After a humorous exchange, he would chuckle with his toothless mouth wide open, giving a cackling sound. More than ever he looked like a merry old owl.

The years passed in ceaseless activity, and Gandhi was approaching seventy. This was an extremely old age by Indian standards. His friends advised him not to overwork himself and to take longer rests, but he paid scant attention to them. Only during the frightfully hot season would he have a cooling mud bandage on his head. "Our mother earth," he would say with a broad grin. "Our mother earth has miraculous properties. That is why I put it on my head, instead of trampling it underfoot."

Gandhi received some of the most famous people of the age in his mud hut, including the representatives of His Britannic Majesty. He welcomed people of lowlier stations, too; people who looked upon him as a sage—even a saint—and upon his dwelling as a tabernacle. His visitors were not only statesmen but also writers, scholars, scientists, and religious leaders—probably the most distinguished gathering in all the world. They sat with him in his cluttered cottage or walked with him, taking care to spare the snakes.

Since Gandhi would not close his door to anyone seeking admission, the ashram often had several unusual people who showed uncommon traits. One of them constantly refused to give his real name, and let himself be called *Banshali*. Once, it was rumored, he had been a college professor who had had a brush with the law and had been jailed for a while. After his release he underwent a strange transformation. He vanished into the forest, reverting to nature, living more like an animal than a man. He lived by sucking the juices of wild fruits, and learned to spot the trees whose leaves he could eat. After his clothing became rags, he wore none. Lacking contact with people, he had forgotten how to speak.

One day Gandhiji found him, took him into the ashram, and nursed him back to life. In time, Banshali regained his capacity to speak and became the hardest-working member of the retreat, spending ten hours daily at the spinning wheel and seven hours at teaching. He also had a good sense of humor, and he liked to entertain other ashramites.

A Japanese *sadhu* (monk) was another interesting dweller at the retreat. He would not kill any living creature under any circumstances, so seriously did he take the obligation of ahimsa. He was the most tireless person in the entire place and no amount of work was too much for him. Word spread that the monk had once been to China to "civilize" its people. Others said that he had been a member of the Japanese espionage world. Gandhi heard about this and said that, in that case, they could use more spies.

A leper was another ashram member. He had contracted the disease in Yeravda jail. Because of his affliction, he had been cast out of his own community and had been on the point of starving to death. He applied to Gandhi, and was admitted.

"I will build a hut for you next to my own," the Mahatma told him. "I am sure you will be the last one to leave me."

Among the distinguished Indians, a frequent visitor was Rajendra Prasad, a top Congress party official and Gandhi's associate for years. Prasad said that being associated with the Mahatma took his mind off his asthma. He did not expect to live long because of it, but he did outlive Gandhi and became his country's first president.

Another visitor was Chakravarti Rajagopalacharia, a man of strong political opinions, good common sense, and strong features. Gandhi's youngest son Devadas later married his daughter, and the marriage strengthened the two men's political bonds. After India's independence, Rajagopalacharia would rise to the high position of first governor general of the country.

Nehru was one of the most frequent visitors. He was

a modern, and Gandhi was a traditionalist. Nehru did not believe in the usefulness of the spinning wheel for India, but in hydroelectric power. India needed large industries, he said, to provide its countless people with employment. But despite these and other differences of opinion, Nehru bowed to Gandhi as his guru—the man who knew India more than anyone else and the man who had the right to speak for all India.

Vallabhbhai Patel, who was to become the nation's first deputy prime minister, also came to see Gandhi, as did the man whom the Mahatma called *Desbandhu*, "the country's brother." He was Chitta Ranjan Das, a prominent political leader from the province of Bengal.

Some of the Mahatma's closest friends were English. One was Charles Freer Andrews, who had been an itinerant missionary in South Africa. He had met Gandhi in 1914, and he remained closely associated with him throughout his life. Reverend Andrews was one of the first to spread the fame of the Great Soul in the English-speaking world. Because of Andrews' deep sympathy for the poor in South Africa and in India, Gandhi called him *Deenabandhu*, "brother of the brotherless."

Other people around the Mahatma were called "young faithfuls." Two of these were Mahadev Desai, his personal secretary, and Nayyar Pyarelal, Desai's successor, the man who "could read the Mahatma's thoughts."

The fame and saintliness of the Mahatma also attracted many women admirers from Great Britain and the United

States. It took much effort on Gandhi's part to convince them that he was not the Messiah whom they had sought.

But some of the visitors were looking for a great man, not a savior. One of them was Madeleine Slade, who had accompanied Gandhi when he sailed to the Round Table Conference. Twenty-three years younger than the Mahatma, she was perceptive and proud, yet humble in serving the great man. She first visited Gandhi in 1925 and stayed with him for life. Gandhi called her *Mirabehn* or *Mira*, his soul companion, adopted daughter, and constant friend. He addressed her in his letters as *Chi. Mira.* *Chi.* is an abbreviation of *Chiranjivi* (long lived), the traditional form of blessing which an older family member bestows on a younger kin. Gandhi revealed more of his "great soul" to her than to anybody else. He recounted his struggles to measure up to the ideal so difficult in human relations—the path to truth.

Besides the greats and the eccentrics whom Gandhi attracted, most of the fellow dwellers in his ashram were honest seekers of truth, who believed, with him, that helpfulness toward others was the solution to all human problems. They found a retreat where everyday petty jealousies were absent in the presence of the Mahatma who saw humanity as the family of all men. While Gandhi's retreat was the powerhouse of India seeking its own identity, it was also more than that. It was a place where human beings could act in a human way.

8

The Search for Peace in War

Gandhi sought truth all through the tragic years that engulfed the world during World War II. Throughout the war, the life story of the Mahatma was completely fused with the life story of India. He no longer had a private life.

What was to happen to India? The Axis powers—Germany, Italy, and Japan—were lined against the Allies —Great Britain and France, and later the Soviet Union and the United States. France was subdued in a matter of days. Germany turned its forces against the Soviet Union in 1941; Japan attacked the United States at Pearl Harbor later that year.

The British had declared war on their enemies in the name of India, without asking the leaders of the subcontinent. Gandhi and the other officials of the National

Congress resented this. Britain had no right, Gandhi said, to wage war in India's name without consulting the nation. Besides, Gandhi added, war would not solve any problem; it never did.

"I appeal to every Briton," he wrote in his weekly *Harijan* on July 6, 1940, ". . . to accept the method of nonviolence instead of war for the adjustment of relations among nations. . . . Your statesmen have declared that this is a war on behalf of democracy. . . . I suggest that at the end of the war, whichever way it ends, there will be no democracy left to represent democracy. . . ."

The Axis powers launched a global offensive: while the Germans swept into the Soviet Union, Japan drove into Asia, defeating the English, the French, and the Dutch and occupying their colonies. A former president of the Indian National Congress, Subhas Chandra Bose, recruited Indians for a pro-Japanese armed force, *Azad Hind* (Free India.) He also formed a "Provisional Government of Free India."

In their stunningly swift advance, the Japanese overran Burma, India's eastern neighbor and a British possession. The conquerors began to scale the mountain peaks separating Burma from India. This was the darkest hour for the British Empire.

Gandhi, above all, wanted independence for his people. This was the time to get it by rising against the British masters. England, engaged in a life and death struggle in Europe, would not be able to subdue hundreds of millions of Indians. Meanwhile the Germans were marching eastward with giant strides, while the Japanese swept westward in a titanic outburst of energy. Their meeting place might be India, long considered the pivot of the British Empire. Was this not the time to make India free without Britain's permission?

The leaders of the Congress party, speaking for the majority of India's people, wanted freedom. But they did not want it with the aid of Germany and Japan. They detested the governmental views of these countries, which the world knew under the name of fascism. It was an extreme form of nationalism, believing in brute strength, exalting war, and glorifying the "races" that it considered superior. Gandhi did not give the signal for India to rise. It would have meant violence, in which he did not believe. Also, an India in revolt would have aided the Fascist cause, which he detested. Yet, he believed that this was the time to press the British government by peaceful means, in order to set India free.

The head of the government was now Winston Churchill, a titanic man of the old school who believed in imperial destiny. Solemnly, Churchill declared that he would not preside over the disintegration of the British Empire. Yet, not even Churchill could take chances with the subcontinent. As the Axis armies raced toward a global junction, India might rise against Britain, even though Gandhi opposed violence. Other leaders might override the Mahatma's wishes. The British knew that they would be unable to crush an uprising, so Churchill decided that the Indians had to be kept quiet.

An admirer of Gandhi and a friend of India, Sir Stafford Cripps, was a prominent figure in the British Labor party and an outstanding member of the British Cabinet. Prime Minister Churchill decided to send Cripps to India early in 1942 with an offer of independence.

India's leaders were eager to hear Britain's proposal and they knew that Cripps was their friend. But this friend was also a member of the British wartime government and the message that he carried was that of his government.

"You will have independence," Sir Stafford told the Indians, "but it will have to await our victory."

Stunned silence greeted this announcement.

Cripps continued. "Countless details will have to be attended to in connection with independence. Your Muslim fellow countrymen, headed by Mohammed Ali Jinnah, want assurance that they will not be swamped by the Hindus and their ideas. They have to be given serious thought. Then there are all your princes with whom we have treaty obligations. We cannot break those treaties. Their problems will have to be solved before independence is declared."

In reply Gandhi told Cripps, "We appreciate your efforts. But you are offering us a postdated check which we cannot accept. The check should bear today's date."

Sir Stafford was not authorized to issue such a "check."

Regretfully, he returned to London, his business unfinished. The British continued to control India, and they recruited volunteers to fight their enemies. They built a large army in the subcontinent consisting mainly of Gurkhas, Sikhs, Kashmiris, and Punjabi, whom they called the "martial races." These soldiers gave an excellent account of themselves.

Again India looked to Gandhi, and he spoke at the next Congress in August, 1942.

The essence of his speech was *karenge ya marenge,* "do or die." He called upon his people to demand that the Allies live up to their pledge included in the Atlantic Charter, signed the year before by the President of the United States, Franklin D. Roosevelt, and Prime Minister Winston Churchill. The pledge said that the signatory governments would "respect the right of all peoples to choose the form of government under which they wanted to live." India, Gandhi said, wanted to live under its own government. Therefore, England should leave the subcontinent. At the same time, Gandhi called upon his countrymen to resume the campaign of satyagraha, civil disobedience against their British masters.

There was again an ominous knock on Gandhi's door the day after he delivered his address. He had anticipated it, and his small parcel of belongings and bedding were ready. This time he was not taken to Yeravda prison, but to the residence in Poona of one of India's richest men, the Aga Khan.

Gandhi was now at a very advanced age and if he had died in a common jail, India would have exploded in revolts. His wife Kasturbai, still active in politics with her husband, was detained with him.

The fact that the Mahatma was a prisoner again cast sorrow and resentment over all the land. The nation was stunned, and then it erupted into savage anger. Months of violent outbreaks paralyzed the country's war efforts. The British government was stern. Again the leaders of the Congress party were jailed in overcrowded cells.

On October 2, 1942—while in detention—Gandhi reached the age of seventy-three. In the Aga Khan's residence, he was visited by countless people, who turned his place of detention into a place of pilgrimage. In spite of his age, Gandhi kept at his work with his accustomed speed. The American writer Louis Fischer was one of his visitors and he described Gandhi as he looked at the time. More than ever before he looked like a wise old owl, with birdlike features and large, round questing eyes. His face formed a small part of his high-domed skull. His upper lip was covered with the black and white fuzz of a moustache. His soft dark eyes revealed an expression of utter gentleness. His toothless mouth seemed to be large in his small face. He used his dentures only for eating. His meal over, he washed them and then put them aside.

"Whether he was speaking, listening or thinking," Fischer wrote, "his face was a twinkling mirror with many facets which reflected what went behind it. He did not attempt to formulate his ideas in finished form: he thought aloud, so one could hear his brain tick. You heard not just words; you heard his thoughts being born."

Another one of his visitors was Rabindranath Tagore. "Perhaps he will not succeed," Tagore meditated after one of his visits. "Perhaps he will fail as Buddha failed, and as Christ failed to wean men from their iniquities; but he will always be remembered as one who made his life a lesson for all ages to come."

People who could not get into the palace just stood in front of it, hoping that his *teja* (blessing) would fall upon them because of the "invisible radiation" of the saintly man.

Although a prisoner, Gandhi was still his peoples' spokesman. On behalf of India, he carried on correspondence with Lord Linlithgow, the Viceroy of India. It was a unique correspondence which covered not only political issues but philosophical and ethical problems, too. In his letters, Gandhi gave his address as "Detention camp" while Linlithgow's stationery said: "The Viceroy's House, New Delhi." Gandhi signed his letters: "I am, Your Sincere friend, M. K. Gandhi," and the Viceroy signed his, "Yours sincerely, Linlithgow."

In his correspondence, Gandhi sought to explain to the viceroy that India did not want Hitler's victory any more than Britain did, but that India thought an Allied victory could best be assured by lining up the subcontinent on

Britain's side as a free nation. The viceroy answered that Gandhi's "Quit India" resolution hurt the Allied war effort and caused violence. This insinuation sorrowed the Mahatma, and he replied that since his policy was ahimsa, he could not see how Linlithgow could justify the charge.

Linlithgow wrote that intention was one thing and action something else. The action of bunglers, he said, often distorted good peoples' intentions.

The two men did not change each other's views through their correspondence because neither of the two would yield a single inch. But London was intent on breaking the deadlock, and *did* yield. Linlithgow received London's orders to return to England for another assignment, an indication that his line had been found too rigid. Before his return, the two men exchanged letters that were unique in India's history.

"On the eve of your departure from India," Gandhi wrote, "I would like to send you a word. Of all the functionaries I have had the honor of knowing, none has been the cause of such deep sorrow to me as you have. It has cut me to the quick to have you think of me as having countenanced untruth, and that regarding one whom you at one time considered your friend. I hope and pray that God will some day put it into your heart to realize that you, the representative of a great nation, has been led into a grievous error.

"With good wishes, I still remain your friend, M. K. Gandhi."

The letter was dated Detention Camp, September 27, 1943.

The Viceroy's answer was marked "Personal, Viceroy's Camp, India (Simla), October 7, 1943," and it read:

"Dear Mr. Gandhi: . . . I am indeed sorry that your feelings about any deeds or words of mine should be as you describe. But I must be allowed, as gently as I may, to make plain to you that I am quite unable to accept your interpretation of the events in question.

"As for the corrective virtues of time and reflection, evidently they are ubiquitous in their operation, and wisely to be rejected by no man.

"I am sincerely, Linlithgow."

During the period of this correspondence, great sorrow came to Gandhi. Kasturbai had two heart attacks in quick succession. The Gandhis had now been married for sixty-two years. For many years they had lived as loving friends, not man and wife. She looked even older than he, although they were the same age. Kasturbai's motto had been, "If you can endure hardships, I can, too." Then she had added, "I want to join the struggle." In his ashram, she had been the "presiding deity." On several occasions she had shared her husband's fate in jail, fighting at his side for their common cause.

After Kasturbai's heart attacks, the doctors and all of India were concerned about her life. Regular bulletins were issued about her condition. The government bulletin on February 20, 1944, announced: "Mrs. Gandhi's condition has been deteriorating for some days past and is now very grave."

Her life was ebbing fast. Devadas, her youngest son, was in her sick room. She fondled his hands, then called for her husband. Gandhi hurried to her bedside, propped her up, and she leaned against him. Tears poured from Gandhi's eyes.

Close friends were hastily summoned, and they began to chant her favorite religious hymns. A faint smile appeared on her wan and wrinkled face, and she died.

Women dressed Kasturbai in a white sari, covered it with an orange-colored homespun *khaddar* sheet, and then anointed her forehead with *kumkum* (vermillion), traditional to the burial rite. Her flower-bedecked bier was transferred to the place of cremation alongside a stream some one hundred yards away. The funeral pyre was arranged and the body placed on it. Gandhi was released from detention and he conducted the services by reading passages from the sacred scripts of three religions: Hindu, Muslim, and Christian. Then sandalwood was piled on Kasturbai's bier. Three times Devadas Gandhi circled the pyre, then set a torch to the sandalwood, which emitted a sweet fragrance.

The cremation over, Devadas collected a handful of ashes and placed them on a canopy of flowers which he held. Then incense was sprinkled on the ashes. Devadas took the ashes and flowers to the Ganges, the Hindu's most sacred river, and immersed them. The funeral rites were over.

Supported by his youngest son, Gandhi returned to his place of detention.

"My father grieves over this tragic gap in his life," Devadas noted, "for she, in a large measure, was responsible for what he is today."

The excitement was too much for Mohandas Gandhi, and after his wife's funeral, he was laid low by malaria, a common ailment in India. While not fatal if properly treated it is an energy-sapping disease. Because of Gandhi's sickness, the British were again in a quandary. If the "Great Soul" died in detention, the country would be shaken with endless riots. And yet the government wanted to keep him in sight.

Viscount Wavell was now the viceroy, and he wished to take no chances with Gandhi's health. On May 6, 1944, he released Gandhi unconditionally. The Mahatma was never again to be jailed. He had spent 2,338 days of his life as a prisoner. Looking back, Gandhi's friends realized that the jail terms had not broken his spirit. On the contrary, they had afforded him leisure to collect his thoughts, to learn more about India and himself, to read, write, and meditate. As in the case of other unusual people, the jail had served Gandhi as a school of higher learning.

From his detention Gandhi emerged into a world that had undergone great changes during his absence of twenty-one months. When he had been jailed, the Allies had been on the defensive at all fronts. But with the turn of 1943, the situation had changed. The Nazis were in retreat on Russia's frozen wastes; they and their Italian allies were also in retreat under North Africa's flaming sun. Soon after Gandhi's liberation, American and British forces landed in western France for their final push. The Nazis were forced back everywhere, and the Italian monarchy left the Axis' side. The war ended in Europe in 1945. Shortly thereafter new weapons of fantastic destructive powers burst upon the two Japanese cities of Hiroshima and Nagasaki. The age of nuclear weapons opened, and the war was over.

Although the British were on the winning side, they had lost their strength in winning the war. No sooner were the hostilities over when the "cold war" began between Communist Russia and its former allies. The Communists now started their anti-West campaign, proclaiming that the majority of the people of the "free world" were not free. The Indians certainly were not. To counteract the Soviets, the United States exerted pressure upon Britain to put an end to this contradiction. In London there had been a change of government. The gigantic figure of the war, Winston Churchill, had been voted out of office, and in came the British Labor party, headed by

Clement Attlee, a friend of India. Many prominent Laborites were in favor of establishing new relations with the subcontinent.

Gandhi thus emerged into a world in which India was to be assigned a new place. The wartime admonition to Britain—Quit India—was now revived. This time Britain had no other choice. But many problems had to be solved before the final step was taken.

Most pressing was the problem of the relations between Hindus and Muslims in a free India—the communal question. It was Gandhi's contention that, irrespective of their religions, the people of India formed a unit.

"Look at the western countries," he reminded the Muslims. There are millions of Catholics in America. Should there be a Catholic U.S.A. and a Protestant U.S.A.?"

In debating this issue, his opponent was the Muslim League spokesman, the tall, lean, aristocratic-looking lawyer, Mohammed Ali Jinnah. At one time, Jinnah had been on Gandhi's side fighting for a united India's freedom within the National Congress. But he had left the Congress party and demanded that India be split between Hindus and Muslims. He adopted a new name for Muslim India—Pakistan. There had never been a country by that name, and the translation meant "Land of the Pure."

Gandhi and Jinnah carried on a correspondence about India's future. The Mahatma addressed Mohammed Ali as "Brother Jinnah," and signed his letters, "Your brother

M. K. Gandhi." Jinnah replied stiffly: "Dear Mr. Gandhi," and signed, "Yours sincerely, M. A. Jinnah."

Gandhi sought to convince Jinnah that it was in the nation's interest to be united. It was an economic unit and people would suffer if it were rent apart. This may be so, Jinnah answered, but the Muslims wanted to have a country of their own. Gandhi replied that in this age religion was no longer a basis for setting up different nations. Jinnah said that while this may be true in the West, in India religions also meant entirely different ways of life. Gandhi argued that the division of the subcontinent would present unsolvable problems. For one thing, India's Muslims did not live in one area, but were scattered all over the land. They formed majorities only in two regions: in the extreme northeast, East Bengal, and in the Northwest, the Punjab. That did not matter, Jinnah answered. Pakistan would then have two "wings." That made no sense, Gandhi replied, because those two wings were a thousand miles apart. How could such a country be governed? It will be governed, Jinnah told him.

"This arrangement makes no sense," Congress party people echoed, including the Muslims within the party. "Why does Jinnah do this? He himself is not even a religious Muslim."

"He does it," the critics replied, "because of Gandhi."

"But the Mahatma is the least aggressive person in the world."

"But he is the best-known Indian in the world."

"What difference does that make to Jinnah?"

"A lot of difference. He is the type of man who does not want to be eclipsed by anyone. If he cannot be 'Mr. India,' which he cannot be because of the Mahatma, he wants to be 'Mr. Pakistan.' He is very proud and vain."

As word spread that Hindus and Muslims were to have countries of their own, communal riots flared up again in sensitive areas. That was nothing new in Indian history, in spite of the fact that Hindus and Muslims lived in peace as neighbors in many parts.

Jinnah proclaimed August 17, 1946, as "Direct Action Day," on which Muslims were to demonstrate in favor of Pakistan. "Direct action" it became in a most tragic way. Five thousand people were killed. The following day, five thousand more were killed in communal riots in Calcutta alone. From there violence spread to other parts of Bengal and to the Punjab. Particularly terrible were the attacks on Hindus by Muslims in the town of Noakhali in eastern Bengal. At the time Gandhi had his residence in New Delhi, but he decided, in spite of his age, to go into the danger area. Noakhali was situated in the all but inaccessible region of the swampy deltas of the Ganges and Brahmaputra rivers. Yet Gandhi got there, and for months toured the area. Everywhere he saw evidence of murder, arson, forcible conversions, and looting. To counteract these explosions of madness, he held evening prayer meetings which were attended by thousands. He admonished his hearers that religion was love, not murder. Trying to make people see sense, he undertook a particularly strenuous tour walking from village to village. Meanwhile the British were busy with their plans. Now they wanted to transfer power quickly and yet in an orderly way. They realized that India had to be split up between a Hindu nation and a Muslim country. There was also the problem of the hundreds of principalities with which they had concluded treaties in the past. In concluding these pacts, the princes had expected to rule under Britain's protective shield. But Britain no longer had a shield. Attlee's government had to advise the princes to make their own arrangements with one of the two new emerging nations. Because of their geographic locations, they would have to accede either to India or to Pakistan. The new governments might provide them with means to live in their accustomed way.

On his tour, Gandhi was in touch with other Congress party leaders, and he continued to oppose the division of India into two nations.

"If the country is divided," he insisted, "the body will be ours, but theirs will be the two arms." Then he added sadly, "What will we do without the arms? What will they do without the body?" This was in reference to the shape of the peninsula after the division: the torso to India; the arms, or wings, to Pakistan.

While negotiations were going on, more outbreaks occurred in East Bengal. The rioting spread to the adjacent province of Bihar, then to West Bengal where the Hindu majority began to slaughter Muslims. The Mahatma used all his resources of persuasion to quiet down the frenzy.

He told the people of Bihar, "You are people of the Hindustan plains, and your lands are watered by the Ganges. It is the river of India which feeds and purifies not only Hindus, but also Muslims, Sikhs, and others. We consider the Ganges sacred, but it cannot remain so if it is polluted by innocent peoples' blood. We must learn to live according to the teachings of the gods of the Hindus, and also of Allah, the Muslim god. You who are Hindus, think of the paeans to peace in the great *Avesta*. And you Muslims, think of your own daily greeting—*salam aleikum*—may you live in peace. We are on the threshold of a new age and a great future. This is the moment for which we had been waiting. Let us now think of our responsibilities, and not besmirch our land with blood. Let us be worthy of our role."

Often the enraptured villages took the ahimsa vow after Gandhi's address. But as soon as he was gone they were at each other's throats again.

In the midst of his travels, an urgent call reached Gandhi to return to New Delhi. Lord Wavell had now been replaced by Lord Mountbatten as viceroy. His only task was to free India. Gandhi was to confer with him in the viceregal residence. The viceroy and the Mahatma did talk at length. Gandhi held out for a united India, but was overruled by his own followers who knew that time was running out. India was to be divided and become independent with no further delay. There was to be a country of Pakistan, its two sections a thousand miles apart.

August 15, 1947, was proclaimed Independence Day. In front of the viceregal residence, eventually to become the *Rashtrapati Bhavan,* or president's house, the Union Jack of Britain was taken down and replaced by the Indian national flag, a tricolor of saffron, white, and green stripes. In the center was Gandhi's own charkha, the hand spinning wheel. India's capital was New Delhi; Pakistan's was Karachi on the Arabian Sea in the distant west. Pakistan's banner bore the Muslim crescent on a field of green, the color of the prophet Mohammed, with a white stripe for the non-Muslims of the new country.

On Independence Day, Gandhi was in Calcutta, where he had gone to stop another outbreak of rioting. Again death stalked the streets of the great city. Gandhi saw bodies in the streets and heard about the frightful flare-ups sweeping other regions of the country in the Punjab. There Muslims and Hindus, hopelessly mixed, also faced a large Sikh population distressed by the fact that it was to have no nation of its own.

The people of India had been hoping for independence for years. Now it was theirs. And yet it was fear—not joy—that gripped their hearts. Fear was also in Gandhi's heart when he realized that the nation he had dedicated to nonviolence was celebrating its birthday with senseless shedding of blood.

9

Tragedy and Independence

There should have been jubilation in the thousands of villages. Instead there was bloodshed. The news that India was to be partitioned spread like wildfire. Millions of people left their homes. Hindus in Pakistan tried to reach India, and Muslims in India tried to reach Pakistan. Nobody knew the exact number of people on the march, but everybody knew that it was the greatest exodus in human history—involving possibly fifteen million people.

It had been a bad summer for India. The monsoon rains were inadequate that year, and more people had starved than in other years. Many were dejected because of the uncertainty of the future. They were gripped by an impulse to leave their mud huts and gutters in the alleys, and move into regions where their religion would be understood, if not their language.

On the dusty roads of the Punjab, an endless column of Muslim refugees headed westward into West Pakistan, and another endless column of Hindus headed eastward into India. The wanderers were miserable travelers, carrying their pots and pans. This was all they had. As the columns met, the people started to fight, then to kill one another. Hindus killed Muslims; Muslims killed Hindus; while the Sikhs killed Muslims and Hindus and were in turn killed by them. They did not kill for money—all were beggars. Why then? They did not know.

Other highways, other villages and towns were the scenes of mass murder. Probably hundreds of thousands of people were killed. The estimates range all the way to one million.

No nations were born in the midst of so much bloodshed as Pakistan and India. This happened in spite of the fact that India's great leader had taught his people to observe ahimsa, no violence, even if attacked. Bloodshed never purifies, he said; it always pollutes.

Perhaps Gandhi had opposed partition because he had foreseen this result. But now partition was an accomplished fact. Even after the mass migrations, about forty million Muslims remained citizens of India and ten million Hindus stayed in Pakistan. Gandhi was fearful for their future safety. What could he do? He would try to head off another outbreak and to ensure a more secure life for the minorities. With that in mind, he organized teams of fellow workers. He told them, "Go among the rioters and keep them from indulging in madness even if you yourselves get killed in the attempt. Don't return alive to report failure. The situation calls for the utmost sacrifice."

Even though he was now past seventy-eight, he decided to visit the most dangerous areas himself. His friends pleaded with him. "Don't go, bapu," they said. "Suppose a madman kills you. Things would get even worse in all India."

"I cannot sit here and wait—I have to do my bit," Gandhi answered. "If I falter now, the frenzy may spread further. And there is another danger, too. If we reveal our weakness at the very beginning of our freedom, great powers may decide to pounce upon us. That would turn our freedom into a short nightmare."

Now that India was an independent nation, Gandhi could have occupied the highest post in the government. But that was not his aim. He wanted no government position, high or low. Younger shoulders than his would have to carry "the bricks and mortars" for the erection of the new state. As an active politician, he would have belonged to only one party. But he was a living legend and thus belonged to *all* India.

His disciple, Jawaharlal Nehru, now rose to the most influential position in the state. Gandhi wanted Nehru in the highest post even though he disagreed with him on important points. Nehru was a socialist; Gandhi was not.

The Mahatma was not much concerned with economics, the most important ingredient of Marxist socialism. But a difference of views did not keep Gandhi from backing Nehru because he considered him the best man in the Congress party. Panditji became the first prime minister of free India.

The new nation remained within the British Commonwealth, but eventually chose a republican form of government. Gandhi did not want the highest decorative position either. Another close associate of his, Chakravarti Rajagopalacharia, became the first governor general of the new nation. Some of Gandhi's other disciples, too, became high officials of the government.

Pakistan also became a reality. Although Gandhi had opposed the severance of ancient ties, he now accepted the Muslim neighbor with good grace.

"No tears should be shed because of the inevitable. Let the past bury the past."

The constitution of the new nation was to reflect the most advanced thought of the age, and India was to become a model of democracy. The dreams of yesterday would be the realities of today. Those realities were incorporated into the constitution of the country which mirrored the thoughts of the Great Soul.

Gandhi wanted Dr. Ambedkar, leader of the untouchables, to draw up the country's constitution, even though Ambedkar had been particularly abusive to Gandhi during their disagreement over separate elections for the Harijans. The Great Soul was not a man to hold grudges. Ambedkar did write the constitution, a broad-minded document providing for special protection for those whom Gandhi called the children of God. Discrimination under the constitution became a criminal offense.

But embers of hatred still smoldered, especially in border areas such as India's most populous city, Calcutta, a few miles from the Pakistani border. Communal riots between Hindus and Muslims erupted again and again. Gandhi went once more to the city with his staff, striding with long steps, and staring with searching eyes.

It was September, 1947. The stifling heat of Bengal had abated, but not the hatred. More than ever before, Gandhiji was dismayed. India was free; people should refrain from enmity and should not kill. What could he do to put an end to this madness? He resorted to his strongest weapon. He offered his own life to end the outbreaks. Gandhi announced that he would fast, which at his age was extremely dangerous.

His disciples implored him not to run this risk, but he was adamant. He returned to his Delhi residence, and while the rioting in Calcutta continued, he began his greatest fast.

"I have embarked on this fast," he told his friends, "in the name of truth whose familiar name is God. Without living truth, God is nowhere. In God's name we have committed massacres and lies, killing women, children, and infants. We have indulged in abductions, forcible conversions, and we have done all this without shame. . . ."

He shouldered his share of the blame.

"It was I who launched the campaign of noncooperation against the British who held us in their thrall. But my noncooperation was nonviolent. And what do I see today? My own people are noncooperating with one another, disregarding our pledge of nonviolence. What is the reason? Perhaps this: I have not been without blame of violence in my own life. Because of my imperfections, I seem to have lost the power to make people heed my words. I blame myself and nobody else; my fasting is a penance. Thus I submit my craven petition to God whose name is truth. If nobody else does, He will listen to me."

His disciples rushed into the riotous area, spreading the news of Gandhi's fast. They exacted pledges of no violence from the people. Gandhi accepted the pledges and broke his fast. He had stopped the riots.

From Delhi, Gandhi now visited Hindu and Sikh refugees from the Punjab. He was always on the move, always imploring people to work together for a better world.

It was now January, 1948, and Gandhi was in his seventy-ninth year. When people pleaded with him not to strain the reserves of his energy, he answered with a twinkle in his eyes, "I do not drink, I do not smoke, I eat very little, I abjured sexual life ages ago. I look frail but have a strong constitution." And then he added with his impish grin, "I expect to be at least one hundred and twenty when I die." People who knew him well said that he meant it, too.

In Delhi, Gandhi was staying in the house of the Birla brothers, industrial and newspaper magnates. Their daily paper, *The Hindustan Times*, was edited by Devadas, Gandhi's youngest son. Communal rioting broke out again as Gandhi rested after his tours. He started a new fast on January 12, 1948. It lasted for five days, until representatives of the Hindus, Muslims, and Sikhs agreed to live in peace.

"I will break my fast," Gandhi said, "trusting your vow that you will be able to stop these mad riots."

He weighed only one hundred and seven pounds when he broke his fast, and the sockets of his dark eyes had sunk deeper than ever into his face. Yet he was in good spirits, and ready, he half joked, "to start life all over again for the next forty years."

The second day after the end of his fast, the Mahatma was up and around, striding to his prayer meetings with his long staff in his hand. He conducted the meetings on the bank of the Jumna River.

In the twilight hours of January 20, 1948, he was conducting the usual prayer meeting. The air was crystal clear, and the western wind blew the pungent scent of the Punjabi desert into the capital.

The meeting was attended by many who adored Gandhi, but scattered in the audience were some who belonged to a new political organization that opposed him. It called itself *Mahasabha*, Great People. The members held that the entire peninsula, including Pakistan, should be merged into one "Greater India." They opposed Gandhi's policy on the ground that he shielded the Muslims.

A loud blast startled the audience in the midst of the meeting. A bomb had been hurled at the platform by a young Punjab refugee, a Mahasabha member who had lost his home because of the partition. The bomb, meant for Gandhi, missed its mark, and he remained unscathed. The Mahatma looked up and told his audience, "Don't worry about that noise; rather listen to me." Then he concluded the meeting as if nothing had happened.

Since it was getting cold, he advised the worshipers, "The January air is getting chill. Next time bring along your straw mats on which to sit, in case you wish to continue these meetings." Then he returned to the Birla House.

The twilight prayer meetings continued, dedicated to reconciling the country's religious communities, which Gandhi considered of the utmost importance for his country's welfare.

On January 30, Gandhi held a conference with Prime Minister Nehru and Deputy Premier Patel. Both Nehru, a socialist, and Patel, who believed in private enterprise, had identical aims—to raise India's distressingly low living standards. Nehru wanted to accomplish it through social action with the government undertaking much of the work; Patel wanted to do it more through individual initiative. Nehru was not opposed to capitalistic economy, and Patel was not opposed to moderate socialism, but they were at odds about the proportions of the two systems. They asked Gandhi's advice, and although they knew that the Mahatma had no broad knowledge of economics, they trusted his intuition. Gandhi expressed his opinion in his usual way.

"Both of you want to attain the same end, to develop the economic life of the country in such a way that people should have more food and more children could go to school. Therefore, I believe that both of you are on the right track. We need people putting their funds into enterprises producing a large variety of goods. But we are a poor country and don't have enough risk capital. America, for instance, has capital accumulations and it has become the most successful capitalist land. We, on the other hand, must organize our society differently, combining the best features of socialism and capitalism. It is right that our entire society—nation—should be working on development problems. Such a social approach has to have socialistic features. Also, it is right that people should risk their own capital for higher profit. Their capital plays a dominant role in capitalism. As I see it, it is best for our country to combine both systems. They are complementary, not competitive."

This was economics in the layman's language. And

these few words were to form the basis for the policy of India, combining the advantages of the public and private sectors, those of government and of private persons.

That evening when the discussion was over, Gandhi had his supper before his public prayer meeting. The two visitors had left. As always, his meal was simple, consisting of a few slices of oranges, goat's milk, ginger juice, and clarified butter, *ghee*.

This time Gandhi was in a hurry, for he was a few minutes late. His disciples had tried to persuade him since the bomb attack to let them stand guard around his platform. He had rejected their proposal, saying that his best protection was God.

A crowd of some five hundred worshipers awaited him. One member of the audience, a follower of the Mahasabha, was violently opposed to India's partition. He was a Hindu, Nathuram Vinayak Godse, belonging to the Brahman caste and a resident of Poona, where he edited a small paper.

Godse had made his way close to the platform on which the Mahatma was conducting the service. He bowed to Gandhi, praying, as he confessed later, that the Great Soul should die without pain. He prayed to his God to help him kill the man whom the world had come to know as the Mahatma. Godse took aim quickly and fired three shots in rapid succession. Gandhi slipped to the ground, losing his spectacles and slippers. As he fell he gasped, *"He Ram,"* (Oh, God).

Worshipers rushed to help him, as others seized the assailant, who offered no resistance. Almost the moment that Gandhi collapsed, he was picked up and rushed to his room in Birla House. His eyes were half-closed but people thought they detected a tiny sign of life. A doctor was called immediately, while his hosts gave Gandhi a heart restorative. The physician arrived promptly, took tests, and then sorrowfully said, "He has been dead for about ten minutes, and nothing on earth could have saved him."

Gandhi's body was laid out in his room in Birla House. The American photographer Margaret Bourke-White visited the room, and later reported: "The women kneeling around the mattress were chanting the name of God, singing *Ram, Ram,* while beating their hands softly to the rhythm of the prayer. Suddenly, into the numbness of that grief-filled room came the incongruous tinkle of broken glass. The glass doors and windows were giving way to the pressure of the crowd outside, straining wildly for one last look at their Mahatma, one last blessing even in death. . . .

"I slipped away from the wordless tragedy of that little room and pressed through a sorrowing crowd to the garden path where Gandhiji met his end. Already a radiance hung over the spot. Someone had marked the place with a candle and its beam was steady and golden in the black Indian night. . . . Kneeling around it were men and women of all religions—just as Gandhiji would have had it. United in deepest sorrow, they were reverently scooping up into their handkerchiefs small handfuls of blood-stained earth to carry away and preserve."

When Devadas, Gandhi's youngest son, arrived half an hour later, he said, "His skin was always tender and smooth to the touch, and naturally beautiful. As I gently pressed his arm with both hands, there seemed to be nothing the matter except that there was no pulse. Sardar Patel and Pandit Nehru sat near him in silence, and many others sobbed as they tried to chant hymns. We kept vigil the whole of that night. So serene was the face and so mellow the halo of divine light that surrounded the body that it seemed almost sacrilegious to grieve."

From all over the world, words of sorrow and sympathy began to flow into Birla House, as Gandhi's body lay in state. Among countless other people, expressions of sympathy came from President Truman of the United States; King George VI, speaking for Britain and other members of the Commonwealth nations; the Soviet foreign minister, Andrei Gromyko; the British Prime Minister, Clement Attlee; Gandhi's antagonist, Mohammed Ali Jinnah; the United Nations and its spokesmen; and other heads of state. They came also from famous individuals: from Mrs. Eleanor Roosevelt, widow of the late President; General Douglas MacArthur; and Nobel Prize winners Pearl S. Buck and Albert Einstein.

The British statesman who had tried to solve India's problem during the war, Sir Stafford Cripps, said in grief,

"I know of no other man of any time . . . who so force-fully and convincingly demonstrated the power of spirit over material things as he."

"Perhaps no man in recorded history," India's Ministry of Information commented, "received such spontaneous tributes of universal praise, reverence, and love as did Mahatma Gandhi at his death."

The sorrow of the entire Indian nation was summed up in Nehru's words: "Friends and comrades, the light has gone out of our lives and there is darkness everywhere."

The day after his death, Gandhi's body was placed on an army weapons carrier hauled by two hundred men of the forces, who used stout ropes. The cortege left Birla House at 11:45 in the morning, and it was two miles long at the time the bier got underway. One million, five hundred thousand people marched in the cortege and another million lined the route. There were people on the tops of houses and on the tops of trees. The destination was the place of cremation on the Jumna River, five and one half miles away. The funeral procession took five hours to cover the distance, and as it reached the river at 4:20 in the afternoon, one million people shouted: "*Gandhi ki-jai*" (to Gandhi victory). People felt that even in his death he was at grips with evil forces. This was a most moving funeral procession.

In accordance with Hindu custom, Gandhi's body was to be cremated and the ashes mingled with India's sacred waters. The funeral pyre of brick, earth, and stone was erected at Pajghat, a short distance from the Jumna. The pyre was eight-feet square, two feet high, covered with sandalwood, and sprinkled with incense. The body of Gandhi was placed on the pyre, his head toward the north, because according to tradition, Lord Buddha died in this position.

Ramdas Gandhi, the third son, performed the final funeral rites, and set fire to the pyre. Quickly the logs burst into flames, and the sandalwood began to spread its fragrance. When they saw the flames, the vast crowd broke into tears. Then, spontaneously, the multitudes pushed through the military lines, surging toward the flames at the crucial moment when the Great Soul was about to be released from earthly bounds. People believed that his blessing at that particular moment would be especially effective. There might have been great injury if the crowd had not been halted at the last minute. Deepest silence followed. After the cremation, the wood continued to smolder for over fourteen hours, during which time traditional prayers were chanted, particularly the *Gita*, Gandhi's favorite religious script. Countless people were unable to tear themselves away from the scene. After the flames had died down, the ashes of Gandhi's body were collected.

The religious rites continued until February 12, thirteen days after the cremation. The ashes were distributed in seven urns to be taken to India's seven sacred streams. First they were sprinkled with sacred water, and then Ramdas wreathed garlands of flowers around the urns.

The ceremony now shifted to the bank of the Ganges, the most sacred of India's streams. The urn that was to be immersed there was placed on a high catafalque, or bier. A special train would carry it to a place below Allahabad, at the junction of the Jumna and Ganges rivers.

When the train left Delhi, darkness had already gathered. The railway passenger car containing the urn was brightly lighted, and millions lined the route, hoping for the final *darshan*. The hands of the people were folded in prayer as they waited in the open fields, at crossroads, and in hamlets and towns all along the tracks. At large places, such as Cawnpore, the train was stopped for some time in order to allow the vast crowd to get the final blessing from the Great Soul.

In a sign of reverence for the immortal dead, bonfires and torches were kept burning in the dark night. After the journey, the train arrived at Allahabad, where close associates of Gandhi awaited the urn, which they carried to the spot where the rivers joined. On its way, the cortege passed the Christian cathedral, and at that very moment the church choir sang one of Gandhi's favorite hymns, "Lead, Kindly Light."

From the city to the place of pilgrimage was a distance of nine miles—nine dusty miles in the dry period of the

Indian year. "The sight was indescribable," wrote an American eyewitness, Vincent Sheean. "All that space filled with people, the greatest concourse of people I have ever seen."

It may have been the greatest concourse of people anybody has ever seen on such an occasion. The size of the crowd was estimated at four million.

At the place of pilgrimage, the ashes were immersed in the sacred waters. This was the final solemn act.

In his memorial address on the site, Nehru said, "The last journey has ended; the final pilgrimage has been made. . . . We shall go away from the riverbank sad and lonely. But we shall also think of the high and unique privilege that has been ours to have had for our chief, leader, and friend, this mighty person, who carried us to great heights on the way to freedom and truth."

The life of Mahatma Gandhi had become a part of history.

10

The Wisdom of the Mahatma
and His Influence

One day the census taker had asked Gandhi about his occupation.

"I am a politician," Gandhi said.

"A politician, bapu? Politicians are supposed to have their moral standards on loose reins."

"Still," Gandhi later reported, "I told him that I was a politician because I concern myself with the public weal. And that is a religious mission. What could be more sacred than the peoples' welfare?"

"Then you consider politics akin to religion?"

"Not merely akin to religion . . . but religion itself. I believe that Divine Providence smiles on people who have learned how to live at peace with their neighbors. And it is the task of the politicians to teach people how to do that."

On another occasion, he had said, "I have one great ambition in life."

"What is it, bapu?"

"To teach people that by hurting others they are hurting themselves. No, that would be wanting too much. I do not mean to say that I want to teach people in general. How could I reach them? I mean some people, the few people I could reach. If I succeeded in that I would feel that my ashes would fertilize the Indian soil."

He said about selfishness: "It is a sickness, and also a sign of weakness. A healthy person knows that his interests are identical with those of his neighbors. He learns from them while teaching them. He sells to them, and also buys from them. . . . The selfish person wants to have all the good things for himself. But if he had everything, he would not need to learn, nor would he have to teach. He would keep everything for himself and would need nothing from others. That would be the end of all education and all trade. Selfishness would thus paralyze two of the most important manifestations of life."

"You also said that selfishness is a sign of weakness."

"Yes, because the weak think they cannot hold their own in the race of life, and so they must have thoughts only for themselves."

"Life is a race then?"

"Obviously. If it were not that, humanity could not exist. The race for survival has made us human."

"But there is a race among the nations, too."

"Naturally."

"Sometimes the race among nations assumes the form of wars. Do you justify them?"

"Certain races among people make no sense and war is an outstanding example. Do you believe that Divine Providence created man so that he should destroy His proudest creation?"

"But there are wars among the lower types of living creatures, too."

"But only man kills his own kind in an organized way, employing his creative forces for destruction—creating mighty engines for mutual extermination."

Then he continued. "Even if you could prove that some animals, such as termites and ants, are capable of organizing wars, the difference between their wars and ours would still be great. Besides, should we take the termites as our models?

"Some people say that man has a death drive, besides the instinct for life, and that wars are instruments of that drive. The human being is the only creature that knows about his inevitable end, and no normal person wants to advance that day. Wars do advance it. I know of people who claim that they do not want to live because life is ugly. That is nonsense. If they think that life is ugly they should try to make it less so.

"These people expect to find a world in which all is harmony and perfection. If the earth had been created harmonious and perfect what do you think would have happened to man? He would not be here at all. He could not have functioned because there would have been no challenge to sustain him. We must have ugliness and other horrid things in life so that we may labor on their removal."

"Will we ever succeed?"

"Obviously, never. Because if we did, life would come to a standstill. But we can work on making life less ugly and horrid, especially if we succeed in removing the institutions that seem to be contrary to God's will, as for instance, the willful and organized destruction of human beings created by Him. That is why nonviolence, ahimsa, is so important."

"You consider it, then, the pivot of all your teachings?"

"Most of my life I have exerted myself to make the few people I could reach realize that ahimsa should be our goal."

"Do you think that the people of India are in a particularly good position to disseminate this knowledge?"

"In a way, yes, although I do not think that ahimsa should be treated as our monopoly. Few people have suffered as much as our people, due to violence among ourselves and on the part of our alien rulers. We should know more about the futility of violence than most other nations. Therefore we should be in a particularly good position to see that it destroys its aims."

"Do you think, bapu, that you are the founder of a new religion, that of no violence?"

"I did not tell the census taker that I was the founder of a religion. I told him that I was a politician. As to ahimsa, you will find the concept of nonviolence in all religions that deserve that name. I merely called attention to it anew, trying to apply it in a particularly violent period of human history."

Gandhi did not found a religion, but he stressed a phase of religious life which many people have over-looked. Thus, not only Indians have come to consider Gandhi as a religious leader. Historians and world leaders have included Gandhi's name with Buddha, Confucius, and Lao-Tse—founders of world religions.

While Gandhi did not claim to be a religious leader, the voice of no other twentieth-century man has been heard by so many millions as his. Contrary to his disclaimer, he *was* a religious leader because he saw politics, too, as the manifestation of man's craving for God on the path of truth. What was his secret? As a youth he had been shy. His physical appearance was far from impressive, and he lacked the strong voice that would attract attention through sheer volume. He was not a good public speaker. He had no official position to lend influence to his words, and he had no wealth. For years he was kept in jails, behind lock and key. Yet, world leaders listened to his weak voice even when he was in jail.

Gandhi had an "inner light," the great English political scientist Harold Laski said. With the aid of that light, he seemed to be able to see truth, not only at a particular time in a particular place, but the truth of the ages. He believed that truth was not merely the opposite of untruth, a one-dimensional affair. It was not something to be recognized in theory and ignored in practice. It was the voice of nature, upon which the balance of the universe was suspended. Nature was truthful, following eternal laws. As long as people were truthful, they were in line with nature's laws. To Gandhi, the pursuit of truth was a dynamic force. He equated it with God, and therefore his quest of it was linked to religion.

That inner light ignited by Gandhi did not burn out with his death. It continued to grow in some of his disciples, who made an attempt to lead Gandhi's consecrated life. Above all, the vast population of India was dedicated to his immortal memory.

A venerated disciple of Gandhi was Acharya Vinoba Bhave, whose fame transcended India's boundaries. It was he, more than any other survivor, who carried on Gandhian policies.

Bhave's lifetime work began during a period of starvation—a situation that afflicts India from time to time. The famine struck three years after Gandhi's death, and it hit the Madras region most severely. Food riots erupted and hungry people said that the famine could have been averted if the landlords had not made food prices too high. Some of the critics were Communists, and a large number of people began to listen to them.

Vinobaji heard about this tragedy. He looked very much like the Great Soul, a wisp of a man with spindly legs. He decided to visit the famine-struck Madras region after the riots, to carry there Gandhi's "inner light."

Vinobaji went to preach Gandhi's ahimsa to the hungry people, so that they would stop their riots against the landlords.

Following Gandhi's custom, he held prayer meetings in the twilight hours after the tropical heat of the day had abated. He saw that many of the peasants were emaciated, and he saw death by starvation, too.

One evening he conducted a prayer meeting in one of the hungry villages of Madras, and he told the peasants that violence would defeat their aim and that they should practice ahimsa. As the peasants looked at him with famished eyes, Vinobaji realized that preaching nonviolence was not enough. Seeing a few landlords in the crowd, he had an inspiration and he turned to them.

"You are able to feed yourselves and your kin," he said, "but look at your neighbors, the landless people. Think of what might happen if in their desperation they set the torch to your land. And think of what might happen if communism came. Your land would be taken away.

"I am telling you that you will be safer if you share some of your land with these hungry people. They will not then lay violent hands on your land, and you will still have more than enough food for your needs. Don't wait until your land is wrested, but give some of it to the poor. Share your food with them and you will be twice blessed."

One of the landlords in the audience, Ram Chandra Reddi, was deeply impressed by these words. Carried away by Vinobaji's eloquent plea, he offered one hundred acres of his land to the village poor. This was the beginning of a movement in the spirit of Gandhi—the *Boodan Yagna* (Land Gift) movement.

Encouraged by this offer, Vinobaji began a campaign that made his name famous throughout the world. He visited countless villages, holding prayer meetings under the night sky, calling upon the landlords to share their surplus with the poor. He told the landlords that he had come "to loot them with love" and that their land donations were in their own interest.

The campaign continued year after year, and in the course of the years Gandhi's disciple collected millions of acres of donated land. While this did not solve the land problem of India, it did show the way to a solution.

Gandhi's influence also spread far beyond the confines of India, especially among the underprivileged people of the world. In the course of time, the name of Gandhiism became synonymous with struggle for justice by nonviolent means. Gandhiism became particularly important in South Africa, where Gandhi had made his mark in his youth, and also among Negroes in the United States.

After Gandhi had finished his work in South Africa, the lot of his countrymen improved for a time. Then again conditions began to deteriorate. The white minority, which ran the country, established a policy of complete segregation known as apartheid—keeping the races completely apart.

In the mid-twentieth century, some three million whites ruled about thirteen million people of other races. The black majority in South Africa found a Gandhian spokesman in Albert John Luthuli.

Luthuli had been the elected native chief of the Zulu tribe in his native town of Groutville in the province of Natal. Luthuli's father had been a Christian missionary, and the son followed Gandhi in considering the Sermon on the Mount as his guide for life. Luthuli realized that he and his people faced a situation similar to Gandhi's. In both cases the minority was strong and ruthless; the majority weak and helpless. He knew that if his people were to be violently aroused against their masters, the result might be wholesale massacre. He also knew that many of his own people would take their oppressors' side because their livelihoods depended upon it. Gandhi's satyagraha became Luthuli's answer to the white minority's apartheid policy.

The aim of the African National Congress, of which

Luthuli became the president in 1951, was to combat apartheid by Gandhi's method. The following year the South African government forced him out of his chieftainship, charged him with high treason, and had him jailed. What was his treasonable act? To claim that all human beings were brothers. "It seems to be treason in South Africa," commented *The Hindustan Times* of New Delhi, "to expect human rights for human beings." Although the charge against Luthuli was too absurd to be pressed, he was forbidden to engage in political activities and forced to leave his home.

In 1961, Luthuli received the Nobel Peace Prize and thus obtained a worldwide platform. He received the recognition because "he always worked with nonviolent methods in the fight against discrimination," in the words of the award.

Another disciple of Gandhi's received the Nobel Peace Prize in 1964. He is an American, Martin Luther King, Jr., an Atlanta-born Negro clergyman. He burst into worldwide prominence when he organized about forty thousand Negroes in a peaceful boycott of bus segregation in Montgomery, Alabama. In 1963 he helped to organize a peaceful march to Washington in protest against racial discrimination. Speaking to nearly a quarter of a million people at the foot of the Lincoln Memorial, his words resounded throughout the land.

"I have a dream," he said to the crowd. This dream was that in the land of the free—the United States—all people should be free, and judged on their merits and not on the color of their skin.

The Nobel Peace Prize committee cited the Gandhian work of the Reverend King as "the first person in the Western world to have shown us that a struggle can be won without violence." Referring to Dr. King's role as leader of the Southern Christian Leadership Conference, the citation described him as the "man who has never abandoned his faith in the unarmed struggle he is waging; who has suffered for his faith; been imprisoned on many occasions; whose home has been subjected to bomb attacks; whose life and those of his family have been threatened; and who, nevertheless, has never faltered."

It was in the name of the "humble children" of the civil rights movement that Dr. King accepted the award. At the same time he announced that he would donate the purse, $54,000, to the civil rights movement. Mahatma Gandhi would undoubtedly have done the same.

Gandhi's disciples received Nobel Peace prizes, but never the Great Soul. His name had been suggested many times, but he never won the prize. Why? Probably because Gandhi had been a British subject, and had fought England's colonial rule first in Africa and then in India. By singling him out for the award, the Scandinavian Nobel Peace Prize committee could have been accused of an insult to the British Empire, which, during that period, was attempting to extend rights to its dependencies.

Gandhi's spirit reigned over the national policies of India, too. Indians agreed that no one but a Gandhi disciple should be entrusted with the task of heading their government. The first prime minister invoked the spirit of the Great Soul in moments of great decisions.

The problems which the Indian government faced were enormous. India is an extremely complicated land, with all its hundreds of tongues, castes, religious practices, and, above all, its abject poverty. The British had done much to improve the people's lot, but it was not enough. Therefore, the government of free India had to launch massive projects to insure a better livelihood for the people, most of whom never had enough to eat.

In dealing with these problems, Indian leaders turned to the legacy left by the Great Soul. How would Gandhi have solved the problem? What had been his view on India's language problem? What would he have done about the castes? What had been his views on economic issues? And his view of democracy? What place would he have suggested for India in foreign affairs?

Gandhi's name was on the lips of Jawaharlal Nehru nearly every time that he set forth government policy.

The problems of building a nation were a great burden for Nehru, and he aged quickly. He died at the head of the government on May 27, 1964, at the age of seventy-four. He was eulogized as the worthiest Gandhi disciple. Darkness descended again on India, just as at the time of Gandhi's death.

Who was to follow in the footsteps of these giants of thought and deed? Who was worthy of carrying on the Gandhian legacy? The decision was made by the Indian National Congress. It selected Lal Bahadur Shastri, who became the second prime minister of India.

Lal Bahadur Shastri had been only sixteen when he had joined the Indian independence movement, and he remained a follower of Gandhi's when he joined the satyagraha campaign. Gandhi and Shastri were jailmates on more than one occasion. Jailed six times, Shastri served seven years in prison. Because of his boycott of British education, Shastri completed his studies in an Indian school of higher learning—Kashi Vidyapith in Benares. He became Congress party secretary in the Uttar Pradesh State. As prime minister, he also invoked Gandhi's spirit in moments of great crisis, bringing a patient approach to the many problems of his country.

Shastri died on January 10, 1966, in Tashkent, Russia, after serving only nineteen months as prime minister. He had gone to the city for a conference with Pakistani leader President Mohammad Ayub Khan, to settle their differences over Kashmir.

Ever since the birth of both countries, they had been in dispute over Kashmir, an Indian state north of the Punjab. The predominantly Muslim population was ruled by a Hindu dynasty. The dispute over control of Kashmir broke into warfare which was halted by the United Nations in 1949. However, the matter was not solved, and serious fighting between India and Pakistan erupted in 1965. In an effort to stop the fighting a conference was initiated by Soviet Premier Aleksei Kosygin. It ended with both countries agreeing to pull back their armies to prewar borders; to reestablish diplomatic relations; and to arrange future conferences to try to settle the problem. Although the Kashmir issue was by no means settled, Shastri had done much for the beginnings of peace.

Shortly after signing the agreement, Shastri suffered his third heart attack in six years, and he was dead at sixty-one. As the Indian people had done for Gandhi and Nehru, thousands joined his funeral procession to the Jumna River.

A few days later, the Congress party leaders selected a new prime minister—one whose name carried great feeling in India. She is Indira Gandhi, daughter of the late Prime Minister Nehru. No relation to the Mahatma, Mrs. Gandhi was married to a lawyer and has two sons. For years she had been a close confidante of her father, and had served Shastri as Information and Broadcasting Minister. A true child of the Indian revolution, she grew up during the years when her parents were constantly being taken off to jail by British rulers, and she was thoroughly imbued with Gandhi's principles of civil disobedience.

"As I stand before you," she said to parliament after being notified of her election as prime minister, "my thoughts go back to the great leaders: Mahatma Gandhi, at whose feet I grew up; Panditji, my father; and Lal Bahadur Shastri."

India has observed Gandhi's policies in selecting its leaders, but has it also observed ahimsa in international affairs? It became a leader of the "non-aligned" countries between the two giants of West and East, the United States and the Soviet Union. Was this a realistic way of practicing ahimsa? As events proved, it did not always work. It did not work in the case of Portugal, which had an enclave in India at Goa. Indian armed forces overran it in 1961. The following year, the Chinese occupied some territories in the high Himalayas to which New Delhi also laid claim. India moved troops up the mountains and a short battle followed. While that may have been self-defense, it was not ahimsa. In 1965, India had a show of force with its neighbor, Pakistan, in the Rann of Kutch, a desolate borderland close to Gandhi's birthplace, and again in Kashmir. These were not manifestations of ahimsa.

What would Gandhi have said to his country, dedicated to nonviolence and now engaged in wars? In the summer of 1965, in the midst of the bloody conflict involving India and Pakistan, some of the most prominent Indians participated in a meeting of the National Committee for Gandhi celebrations. The president, Sarvepalli Radhakrishnan, said, "Truth in action is ahimsa. In practice, it is the doctrine of nonviolence. But it does not ask

us to abstain from force always. When Gandhi talks
about ahimsa, he means by it that we should overcome
evil, restrain it by love. But it was not abstention from
force; it was abstention from hatred."

What would Gandhi have said to this interpretation
of ahimsa? Would he have said, "Don't kill people in
hatred! Kill them in love!"

The answer seems to be that nations have not found
the way to nonviolence, not even Gandhi's people.

Admirers of the Great Soul would like to believe that
he meant a different type of nonviolence, which would
not employ force even in the "spirit of love." Gandhi
believed in the best features of his Hindu religion, which
he expressed in the following words:

"I used to say that I believe in God. Now I say that I
believe in truth. God is truth—that is what I used to say.
Today I say that truth is God. There are many who deny
God, but none denies truth." But the truth that he had
in mind was won by peaceful means.

The *Bhagavad Gita*, Gandhi's favorite classic, contains
a much admired admonition of the Lord Krishna. People,
Krishna said, should practice the *bakhti yoga*—loving devotion. That in turn should be followed by the *kama
yoga*, resolute action, and that—in the interpretation of
the Great Soul—was to combat man's base instincts, his
pugnacious nature, and ultimately to find his peace in
peace.

Gandhi followed the best examples of the great Hindu

teachers. In his youth, he devoted much of his energy to his family. But the sages always said that the just man should enlarge the field of his activities and work for the greater good of a greater number of people. This required abstinence from bodily pleasures and concentration on high aims. Gandhi reached the highest stage, that of the ascetic to which the great Indian teachers pointed as the self-realization of the just man.

India claims Gandhi as its inspiration. Yet, it has been involved in several minor wars, and Hindus and Muslims have still not solved their differences. Does this mean that Gandhi succeeded only in making his people more hypocritical, professing one creed and practicing another? It does not seem so, for Gandhi's teachings hold true. They form vital parts of the intentions which—one hopes—will one day be parts of the normal life of man. Eventually people may have to recognize the most basic truth in Gandhi's teachings: "Violence may achieve its limited aim in the short run but it never solves long run problems."

A long time may pass before Gandhi's real achievements will be realized. Should that time come, he will receive not only respect but also recognition for the actions that he inspired as the Mahatma of India, and also as the immortal constructive soul of the world.

Chronology

1869   October 2—Mohandas Karamchand Gandhi born, Porbandar, India.

1876   Betrothed to Kasturbai.

1881   Enters high school in Rajkot.

1882   Married to Kasturbai.

1886   Father dies.

1888   First son, Harilal, born. Sails to England in September.

1891   Admitted to the bar in London. Returned to India in the summer. Began law practice in Bombay and Rajkot.

1892   Second son, Manilal, born.

1893   Sails for South Africa in April.

1894   Prepared to return to India but remains to do public work.

1896   Returns to India for six months to bring back wife and sons.

1899   Organizes Indian Ambulance Corps for British in Boer War. Third son, Ramdas, born.

1900   Fourth son, Devadas, born.

1903   Opens law office in Johannesburg.

1904   Organizes his first *ashram*, Phoenix Farm, and establishes *Indian Opinion*, a weekly journal.

1906   First satyagraha campaign against "The Black Act" —ordinance to have all Indians fingerprinted and registered.

1908   Sentenced to two months in jail (his first imprisonment). Another *satyagraha* campaign against The Black Act.

1910   Establishes second *ashram*, Tolstoi Farm, near Johannesburg.

1913   Third *satyagraha* campaign against various discriminations. Arrested three times in four days and sentenced to jail. Released in expectation of compromise which became known as "Indian Relief Act."

1914   Leaves South Africa for India by way of England.

1915   Settles in India, engaging in social work against discrimination, especially for the "untouchables."

1915   Opens third ashram, *Satyagraha Ashram*.

1919   England announces "Rowlatt acts," withdrawing civil liberties. Gandhi organizes *hartal*—suspension of all activity after British massacre hundreds at protest meeting of acts.

1919   Begins publication of militant weekly, in English and Gujarati languages, which strongly underscores work of the Congress.

1922   Arrested on charge of sedition, given six-year sentence in Yeravda jail.

1923   Writes *Satyagraha in South Africa* and part of his autobiography while in jail.

1924   Is released from jail, and undergoes surgery for appendicitis. Fasts for twenty-one days. Presides over

Indian National Congress party as its president in December.

1928 Moves resolution for India's independence within one year at the Calcutta session of Congress.

1930 Famous "Great Salt March" from the *Satyagraha Ashram* to the sea—March 12 to April 6. Arrested on May 5.

1931 Released from jail in January. Signs pact which ends campaign of civil disobedience. Participates in Round Table Conference in England.

1932 Jailed again. Begins "fast unto death" against separate electorate, which he considered as discrimination against untouchables.

1933 Fasts against discrimination. Imprisonment for civil disobedience acts.

1934 Retires as president of Indian National Congress. Uses weekly periodical, *Harijan,* to fight problem of discrimination.

1935 Provinces of British India given native governments. Britain remains in over-all control.

1936 Settles in Segaon in his ashram, which is later renamed *Sevagram.*

1940 Protests Britain's action of declaring war in India's name.

1942 Confers with Sir Stafford Cripps about India's status. Sponsors the Congress party's resolution calling on Britain to quit India. Jailed in the palace of Aga Khan near Poona.

1944 Kasturbai dies at the age of seventy-four on February 22. Gandhi is released from imprisonment because of impaired health on May 6.

1946 Confers with British cabinet mission about status

of India. Begins four-months village tour in East Bengal to quell communal riots.

1947 Begins a similar tour in Bihar in March. Begins conferences with Lord Mountbatten, British representative, and Mohammed Ali Jinnah, spokesman of the Indian Muslims. Opposes decision of the Congress to accept a partitioned India. India partitioned and granted independence by the British on August 15.

1948 Bomb explodes at his prayer meeting in Delhi on January 20. He is unhurt. January 30, Hindu fanatic assassinates him in the midst of prayer meeting.

Bibliography

A selected list of Gandhi's works:

Speeches and Writings of Mahatma Gandhi, introduction
    by C. F. Andrews. Madras: Natesan Publishing
    Co., 1934.
The Story of My Experiments with Truth. Washington,
    D.C.: Public Affairs Press, 1948.
Young India. New York: Viking Press, 1927.
Satyagraha in South Africa, translated by Valji G. Desai,
    revised edition. Ahmedabad: Navajivan, 1950.
Songs from Prison, adapted by John Hoylan. New York:
    The Macmillan Co., 1934.
Nonviolence in Peace and War. Ahmedabad: Navajivan
    Vol. I, 1942; Vol. II, 1949.
Communal Unity. Ahmedabad: Navajivan, 1949.
To the Students. Ahmedabad: Navajivan, 1949.
Hind Swaraj. Ahmedabad: Navajivan, 1938.
Satyagraha: Nonviolent Resistance. Ahmedabad: Navaji-
    van, 1951.
The Removal of Untouchability. Ahmedabad: Navajivan,
    1954.
Truth is God. Ahmedabad: Navajivan, 1955.

A selected list of works about Gandhi:

Andrews, C. F. *Mahatma Gandhi's Ideas*. London: Allen and Unwin, 1929.

———., editor. *Mahatma Gandhi: His Own Story*. London: Allen and Unwin, 1930.

Bourke-White, Margaret. *Halfway to Freedom*. New York: Simon and Schuster Inc., 1949.

Catlin, George. *In the Path of Mahatma Gandhi*. London: Macdonald, 1948.

Datta, Dhirendra Mohan. *The Philosophy of Mahatma Gandhi*. Madison: University of Wisconsin Press, 1953.

Duncan, Ronald, editor. *Selected Writings of Mahatma Gandhi*. Boston: Beacon Press, 1951.

Fischer, Louis. *The Life of Mahatma Gandhi*. New York: Harper & Bro., 1950.

———., editor. *The Essential Gandhi*. New York: Random House, 1962.

Gregg, Richard B. *The Power of Nonviolence*. Philadelphia: J. B. Lippincott Co., 1934.

Holmes, John Haynes. *My Gandhi*. New York: Harper & Row, 1953.

Jack, Homer A., editor. *The Gandhi Reader*. Bloomington, Ind.: Indiana University Press, 1956.

———., editor. *The Wit and Wisdom of Gandhi*. Boston: Beacon Press, 1951.

Masani, Shakuntala. *Gandhi's Story*. New York: Oxford University Press, 1950.

Maurer, H. *Great Soul: The Growth of Gandhi*. New York: Doubleday & Co., Inc., 1948.

———. *Mahatma Gandhi: Peaceful Revolutionary*. New York: Charles Scribner's Sons, 1952.

Bibliography

Nehru, Jawaharlal. *Jawaharlal Nehru: An Autobiography.* London: John Lane, 1936. Also under title *Towards Freedom.* New York: The John Day Company, Inc., 1941.

Peare, Catherine O. *Mahatma Gandhi.* New York: Holt, Rinehart & Winston, Inc., 1950.

Reynolds, Reginald. *To Live in Mankind: A Quest for Gandhi.* New York: Doubleday & Co., Inc., 1952.

Rolland, Romain, *Mahatma Gandhi: The Man Who Became One with the Universal Being.* New York: Century House, Inc., 1924.

Sheean, Vincent. *Lead, Kindly Light.* New York: Random House, 1949.

Shridharani, Krishnalal J. *The Mahatma and the World.* New York: Duell, Sloan and Pearce, 1946.

Thomas, Norman. *Great Dissenters.* New York: W. W. Norton & Co., 1961.

Walker, Roy. *Sword of Gold: A Life of Mahatma Gandhi.* London: Indian Independence Union, 1945.

Index

214

Index

Index